THE WORLD OF SCIENCE
COMPUTERS:
AN INTRODUCTION

THE WORLD OF SCIENCE
COMPUTERS:
AN INTRODUCTION

ROGER FORD & OLIVER STRIMPEL

Facts On File Publications
New York, New York • Bicester, England

COMPUTERS: AN INTRODUCTION

First published in the United States of America in
1985 by Facts on File, Inc., 460 Park Avenue South,
New York, N.Y.10016

First published in Great Britain in 1985 by Orbis
Publishing Limited, London

**Library of Congress Cataloging in Publication
Data**

Main entry under title:

World of Science

   Includes index.
   Summary: A twenty-five volume encyclopedia of
scientific subjects, designed for eight- to twelve-year-
olds. One volume is entirely devoted to projects.
   1. Science—Dictionaries, Juvenile.   1. Science—
Dictionaries
Q121.J86   1984   500   84-1654

ISBN: 0-8160-1061-7

Printed in Italy
10 9 8 7 6 5 4 3 2 1

Consultant editors
Eleanor Felder, former managing editor, *New Book of
Knowledge*
James Neujahr, Dean of the School of Education, City
College of New York
Ethan Signer, Professor of Biology, Massachusetts
Institute of Technology
J. Tuzo Wilson, Director General, Ontario Science
Centre

Previous pages
Highly magnified view
of part of the
integrated circuit of a
microprocessor.

Editor Penny Clarke
Designer Roger Kohn

CONTENTS

Note There are some unusual words in this book. They are explained in the Glossary on pages 60–63. The first time each word is used in the text it is printed in *italics*.

◄ Coming in to land your aircraft – or are you? In fact this is the 'pilot's' control panel and view from the 'cockpit' on the monitor screen of a flight simulator.

WHAT IS A COMPUTER?

▼ To get the most out of a computer it needs peripherals – accessories that increase the computer's ability to do things, whether it is play a different type of game or do a more complex set of business calculations. All computers need peripherals such as printers, disk drives and display screens, but you won't find joysticks and trackballs on the huge mainframe computers used by international business corporations!

Printer
A printer is required when paper copies of programs or printed results from the computer are needed. There are several different types of printer; the price reflects the speed and quality of printing

Disk Drives
Like cassettes, disk drives store programs. Instead of a cassette, a 'floppy disk' is used. Disk drives are much more expensive than cassette recorders but they store more information and work much faster. Generally, disk drives are necessary for business computing

Cassette Recorder
The domestic audio cassette recorder provides a low-cost way of saving programs. The program is stored in the computer's memory while the computer is using it. When the power is switched off the contents of this memory disappear. Before this the program can be recorded on audio cassette tape, and played back into the computer when it is needed again

Television
An ordinary television set allows the computer to display messages. And when you are writing programs, anything you type at the keyboard will also appear on the screen. The monitor shown behind the television is designed to give better-quality pictures with more detail

Track Ball Controller
This is used to play games. By rolling the ball in its holder a game piece can be moved around the screen. It provides much finer, faster, more accurate positioning than joysticks and is more comfortable in use. Buttons are provided for firing 'lasers' and so on

The Computer
The computer is the heart of the computer system, though it needs 'extras' to help it communicate with the user. It has a keyboard similar to that on a typewriter, but with some extra keys. Several sockets are provided (usually on the back of the computer) to connect it to other machines such as the cassette recorder or disk drive and the television set

Joystick
These are similar to the controls found on some arcade games. Their actual use depends on the game being played with them. They might control a spaceship or a character in a maze, for example. Some joysticks have a 'pad' of 10 or more buttons (set out like a calculator); how these are used again depends on the game being played

A COMPUTER IS...

A computer is a machine that stores and works with information. It can make decisions about that information and then carry out these decisions. It is this ability to make decisions and then act on them that makes a computer so very different from other machines.

A computer does not have moving parts like other machines – cars or bicycles, for example, that have rods and pistons that go up and down, or wheels that go round. The computer's 'moving parts' are some of the tiniest particles known to man. They are called electrons and are so small that you cannot see them even through the most powerful microscopes. Electrons are responsible for the force we call magnetism. Magnetism lines up the tiny electrons in some metals (usually iron) so that they all point in the same direction. Used in a computer this effect allows us to store information permanently.

For short-term storage, on the other hand, we use an electronic switch called a *transistor* and the computer will store information only as long as the switch allows an electric current to flow.

Computers use both these methods of storing information – to a computer a bit of information is either there, or it's not, just as a light switch is either on or off.

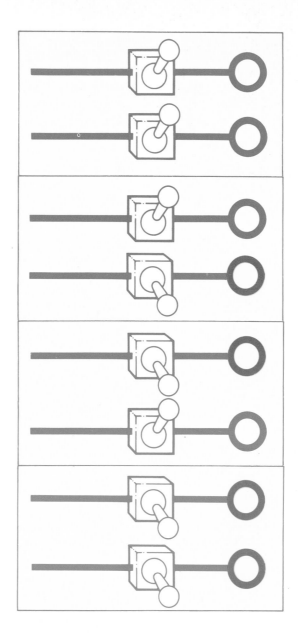

◄ Computers use electrical circuits to represent numbers. The circuits consist largely of switches. A switch may be either on or off. Two switches together can make four combinations of on or off as the diagram shows. Computers use a system like this to represent numbers. Off/off is zero, off/on is one, on/off is two and on/on is three. Using groups of more than two switches means larger numbers can be represented. Computers have thousands of microscopic switches – that is how they can do complicated calculations so quickly.

Programming
A computer on its own is just a lot of electrical circuits, each one able to do a job. We could say the same of a digital wrist-watch, though, so what is the difference? A digital wrist-watch only does one job. It tells the time. It does this by counting off the time second by second, minute by minute, hour by hour and so on. When this watch was designed and made it was 'told' to do just that, and nothing else. Telling a machine what to do is called 'programming', and when we talk about programming a computer we really mean that we are giving it a series of instructions about how to do a job.

Simple decisions
Unlike the digital wrist-watch a computer seems to decide for itself what it will do next. How does it do this? The position of a light switch gives us one piece of information – either there is electricity flowing around the circuit which that switch controls, or there is not. And that electricity, as well as providing the power to light a lamp also tells us something. If there is electricity flowing, then the switch that controls the circuit must be on. The two events are linked together. It is by this method that a computer can seem to decide: If this, then that. It is the fact that computers can make these decisions very, very fast that makes them so useful to us.

► One of IBM's biggest mainframe computers. It is used by large businesses such as banking and insurance.

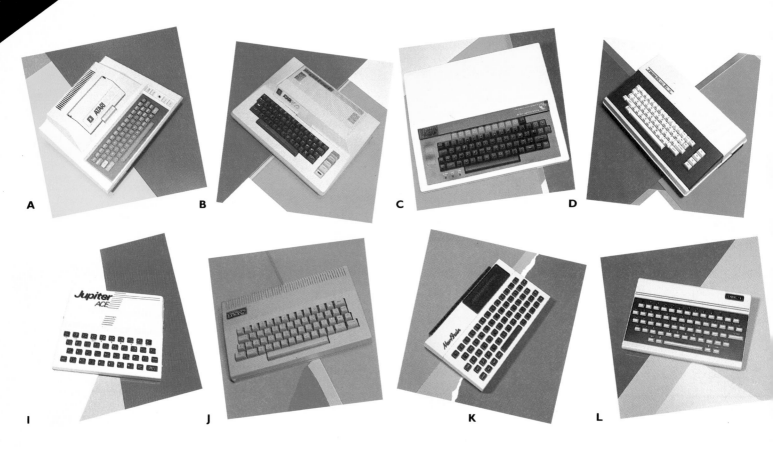

▲ Small computers for the home come in great variety as the manufacturers try to beat their rivals to be the first to get better/cheaper/more sophisticated models on to the market. Although, basically, most models are similar, generally speaking the more expensive the model the better it is – in the same way that the more you pay for a car the better it is likely to be. These are a few of the models available:

THE PARTS OF A COMPUTER

We know (page 7) that a computer is a machine that works with information: storing it, making decisions about it and then acting on those decisions. But a computer is a machine and yet it gets its information and instructions from humans. How do the two work together?

To use a computer we take information in a form understood by humans, feed it into the computer in a way that the computer will understand. Then, when the information (or data) has been processed by the computer, the results are converted back into the form that we humans understand.

To achieve this all computers, whether they are huge *mainframes* or small home computers, have three basic units: an *input* unit, for example the keyboard; a processor unit, this is the *microprocessor* in home computers; and an output unit such as a Visual Display Unit or *VDU*.

▲ A chess-player such as this is a highly sophisticated version of a home computer. This machine has magnets so that the human playing chess with it does not even have to move the pieces!

E

F

G

H

M

N

O

P

A Atari 400, **B** Atari 800, **C** BBC Micro, **D** Colour Genie, **E** Commodore 64,

F Commodore Vic 20, **G** Dragon 32, **H** Epson HX20, **I** Jupiter Ace, **J** Lynx, **K** New Brain,

L Oric, **M** Sinclair ZX81, **N** Sinclair Spectrum, **O** Sord M5, **P** TI 99/4A.

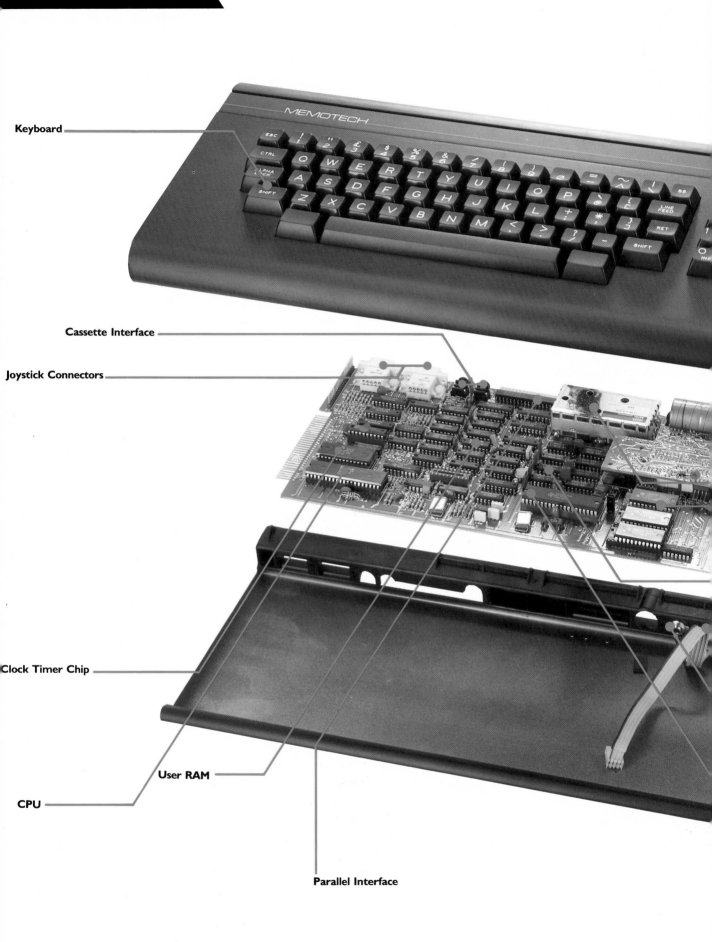

Keyboard

Cassette Interface

Joystick Connectors

Clock Timer Chip

User RAM

CPU

Parallel Interface

▼ Exploded diagram of the Memotech MTX512, showing the different parts of a fairly typical home computer. You can see the QWERTY layout of the keyboard very clearly. The machine has a RAM of 64K (page 26). Don't, however, try taking apart a microcomputer, or indeed any type of computer. You may be able to take it to pieces quite easily, but its the putting back together that is the really difficult part – and the maker's warranty or guarantee does not cover damage of that kind!

Power Connector

RF Modulator

ROM

Video RAM

Monitor Socket

Hi-Fi Connector

Graphics Chip

The keyboard

The most popular way of entering (putting) data into a modern computer is to use a keyboard that looks similar to a typewriter. The keys are laid out in the *QWERTY* pattern, that was devised in the United States in 1873 by two men named Henry Sholes and Christopher Gliden. The user simply types in the information or data that the computer needs.

Chips

The heart – or perhaps we should say 'brain' – of a *microcomputer* is a small flake or '*chip*' of silicon, perhaps 6 mm ($\frac{1}{4}$ in) square, that contains the hundreds of thousands of electronic circuits needed to make the computer. Even a 'microchip' as complex as that is too small to handle comfortably, so it is encased in plastic and fitted with metal legs, which connect it with other microchips so that it looks rather like some kind of big black insect. There are hundreds, maybe thousands, of different sorts of microchips or *Integrated Circuits* (ICs) to give them their technical name. Without magnification they all look very much the same, although they differ in size and in the number of connecting pins they have.

The ALU

The most important part of the microprocessor is the Arithmetic and Logic Unit or *ALU*. The ALU contains the electronic circuits that actually do the work of adding and subtracting numbers and making *logical* decisions based on the information stored in the rest of the computer. You'll remember that this was the most important part of the definition of the computer – a machine that can process information, make logical decisions based on that information and then act on them.

▲ This is an EPROM chip – that is an *E*rasable *P*rogrammable *R*ead-*O*nly *M*emory chip. Anything contained in the chip's memory can be erased with ultraviolet light and new information recorded.

▼ In diagrammatic form, this is what the CPU (Central Processing Unit) of a computer looks like. The ALU (Arithmetic Logic Unit) carries out arithmetical and logical operations. The Control Block accepts the coded instructions (in binary form), interprets them and makes the other parts of the CPU behave according to the instructions. The number of registers in the CPU depends on the type of microprocessor. Registers store the information on which the microprocessor is working. The Stack Pointer and Program Counter work together to take program instructions and data to and from the computer's memory.

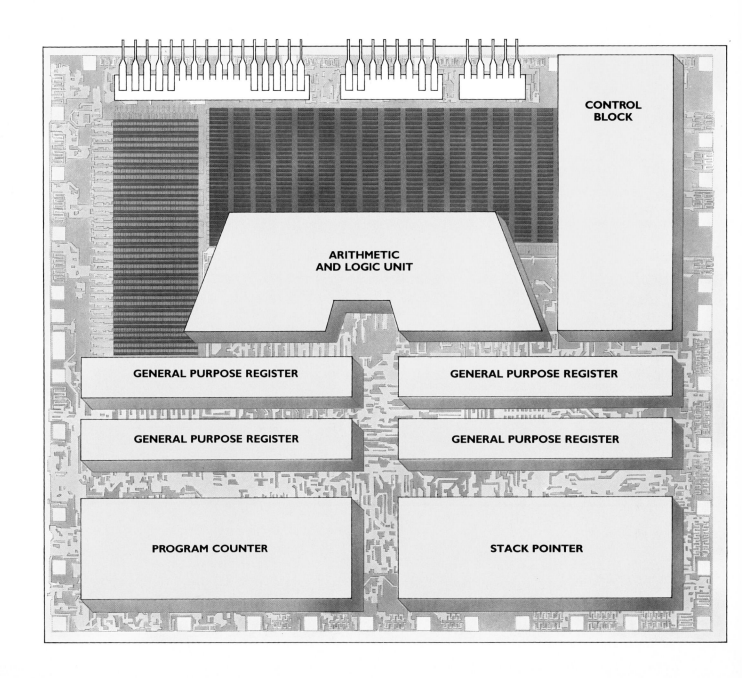

CONTROL BLOCK

ARITHMETIC AND LOGIC UNIT

GENERAL PURPOSE REGISTER

GENERAL PURPOSE REGISTER

GENERAL PURPOSE REGISTER

GENERAL PURPOSE REGISTER

PROGRAM COUNTER

STACK POINTER

Registers

In order to make decisions based on information, there must be somewhere to store that information. Microprocessors have a small amount of storage space, just enough to hold the information they are working on at any one time. They are called *Registers*, and may be one *byte* or two bytes big, depending on the job they're going to do. (Bytes are explained on page 26.)

There is one rather special register called the *Accumulator*. All the information being processed by the computer passes through the Accumulator. The overall number of registers varies according to the type of microprocessor, but this makes no real difference to the computer user provided the program is in a *high-level language* such as *BASIC* (page 29).

Another important part of the microprocessor is a Register that controls the sequence in which *program* instructions will be executed. Not surprisingly, it is called the Sequence Control Register or Program Counter! It is not much more than a counter, keeping a check on the position in the program that we have reached, and deducing from the instruction being executed the position in the *memory* of the next one.

Memory

As well as the microprocessor, the computer needs two other components – memory and support chips. We use two different types of memory inside the computer for different jobs. The memory that holds the program we are running, and the information that that program is using, is temporary – it will be lost if we turn the computer off or reset it. This is called Random Access Memory, or *RAM*. The computer can both read information from it and store information in it. The second type is called Read-Only Memory, or *ROM*, and this is permanent. Even when we turn off the power to the computer the information contained there will stay. It is used to hold things like the BASIC interpreter, the *Operating System* and the *character* set that will be displayed on the screen or printed on the *printer*.

◄ Another type of EPROM – the type of chip that can be re-programmed when ultraviolet light is allowed to pass through a silica 'window' and into the chip's interior to erase whatever information is stored there.

Support chips

The support chips are rather similar to simple microprocessors, but they are 'dedicated' to a particular job, for example controlling the way information comes into, or goes out of, the computer. We, cannot change the way in which they work because they are 'built-in' to the way the computer works. Although they also contain memory of their own (normally called '*buffers*'), their purpose is to store information put out by the microprocessor (a very fast process) while it is waiting to be sent to much slower-acting devices such as the screen, the printer or the *cassette* unit. If the microprocessor had to wait while each character it sent to the printer was actually being produced on the paper, it would be doing nothing for almost all the time!

Displaying the results

If information is put into the computer, there must also be a way of getting it out. Since microcomputers first appeared in the mid-1970s the most common way has been to use a cathode ray tube of the kind used as picture tubes in television sets. In fact, most microcomputers produced for the home use the household TV set to display their results. The computer is plugged into the socket that would normally take the aerial and the computer produces signals that are similar to the ones that make ordinary TV pictures.

Screen Grid

To ensure that the electron guns are pointed at exactly the right place on the screen, a grid or mask is incorporated into the surface of the tube

Screen Phosphor

The coloured image is made up (as shown in the diagram) of three colours. Different substances are laid on the glass. When irradiated by the electron beam, they glow in either red, green or blue, thus giving the coloured image, depending on the intensity of the beam at that point.

Electron Beams

There are three electron beams in the tube, each of which 'excites' a different phosphor to produce a coloured dot

Controls

As on a television, there are various controls. Vertical and horizontal hold are commonly accessible to the user. Colour intensity and other variables are usually not meant to be adjusted and are kept under the cover

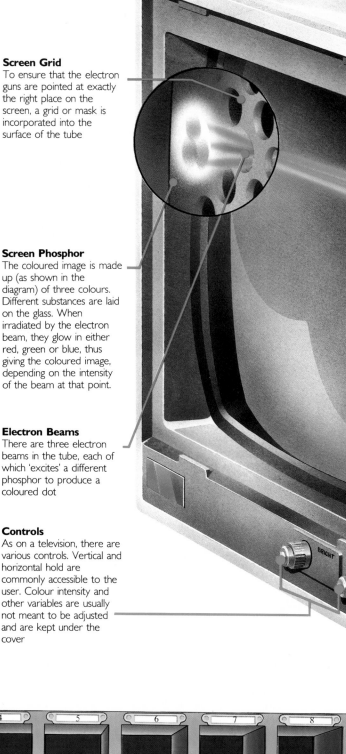

▼ In very simple form, this is how programs are recorded on tape. Every bit from each byte (group of eight bits) is recorded in sequence, one after the other. When the tape is replayed, the computer 'reads' each bit, but stores them as bytes in each memory cell. The first byte on the tape is placed in the first available memory cell, the second in the next one and so on.

▶ A colour monitor works in the same way as a colour television. It just lacks the tuner.

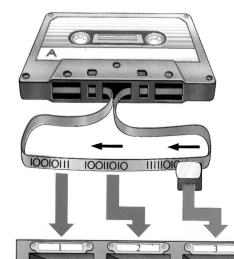

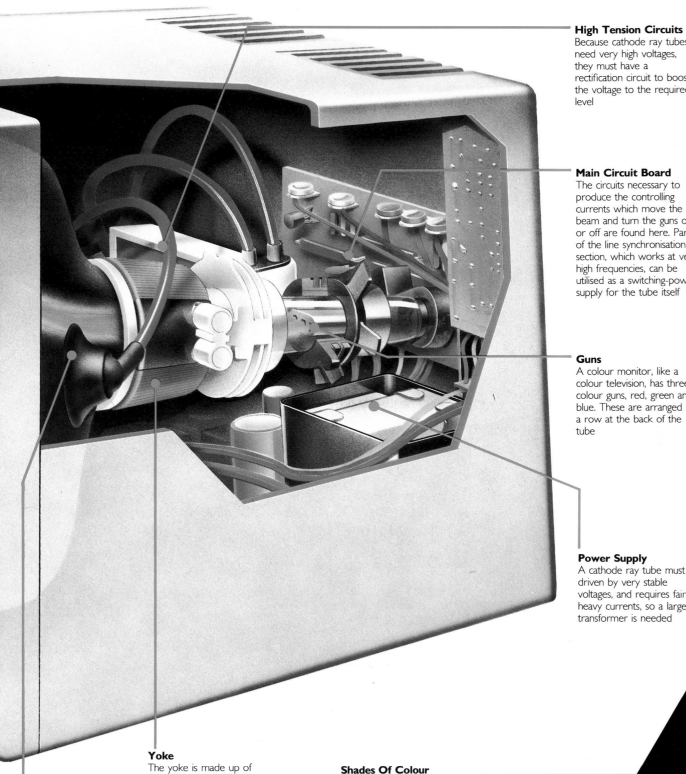

High Tension Circuits
Because cathode ray tubes need very high voltages, they must have a rectification circuit to boost the voltage to the required level

Main Circuit Board
The circuits necessary to produce the controlling currents which move the beam and turn the guns on or off are found here. Part of the line synchronisation section, which works at very high frequencies, can be utilised as a switching-power supply for the tube itself

Guns
A colour monitor, like a colour television, has three colour guns, red, green and blue. These are arranged in a row at the back of the tube

Power Supply
A cathode ray tube must be driven by very stable voltages, and requires fairly heavy currents, so a large transformer is needed

Yoke
The yoke is made up of several large coils that produce powerful magnetic fields. These vary rapidly, so that the dot on the phosphor is moved about, producing the picture

Anode Attachment
Once the beam is ejected from the guns, it is accelerated by the high voltage field. This must be at the other end of the tube and is applied by means of this large, heavily insulated plate, which is on the end of the cable

Shades Of Colour
When sunlight is passed through a glass prism it is separated into a rainbow – or spectrum – stretching from red at one end, through green, to a blue-violet at the other. If this spectrum is then passed through another prism, similar to the first, the colours recombine to give the original sunlight (often called 'white light'). This process of recombination or addition is used in a colour monitor. By adding different strengths of the three main colours, red, green, blue, every colour can be created.

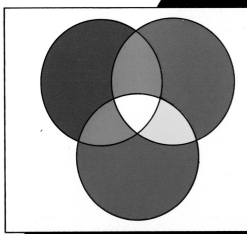

Printed Circuit Boards

No one has yet produced a complete computer on just one chip (although it will probably not be long before they do), so we have to find a way of connecting all these separate components together. The method used is called a *Printed Circuit Board* or PCB. Invented in the United Kingdom in the 1950s, PCBs are now found in all sorts of electronic devices, from toys to TV sets and washing machines to cars. Once the design has been worked out they can be produced automatically, and they allow components to be placed very close together.

It is important that components can be close together for two reasons. First, it means that the computer can be smaller. Second, the connections between one integrated circuit and the next can be made much shorter. This feature is important because modern ICs can work so quickly that the length of time a signal takes to go from one to another can slow the workings of the computer – even though electronic signals travel at the speed of light, which is 299,500 km (186,000 miles) per second!

Operating System

There is another and very important part of the computer that you cannot actually see, but if it wasn't there the computer could not work. This is called the Operating System. It is part of the computer's *software*, in contrast to the parts we've just been describing which are the machine's *hardware*, so there will be more about it in Chapter 6 which deals with software.

The mass of electronic circuits that make up a computer are not much use until we can put information into them and get results out.

▶This photograph shows the PCB (*Printed Circuit Board*) of a Commodore 64. (The keyboard and casing have been removed.) All the individual parts that go to form the computer as a whole are clearly visible.

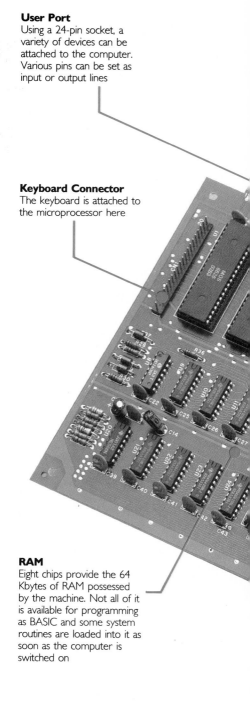

User Port
Using a 24-pin socket, a variety of devices can be attached to the computer. Various pins can be set as input or output lines

Keyboard Connector
The keyboard is attached to the microprocessor here

RAM
Eight chips provide the 64 Kbytes of RAM possessed by the machine. Not all of it is available for programming as BASIC and some system routines are loaded into it as soon as the computer is switched on

Microprocessor
It controls all the operations of the computer as well as handling a good deal of the input/output

Sound Chip

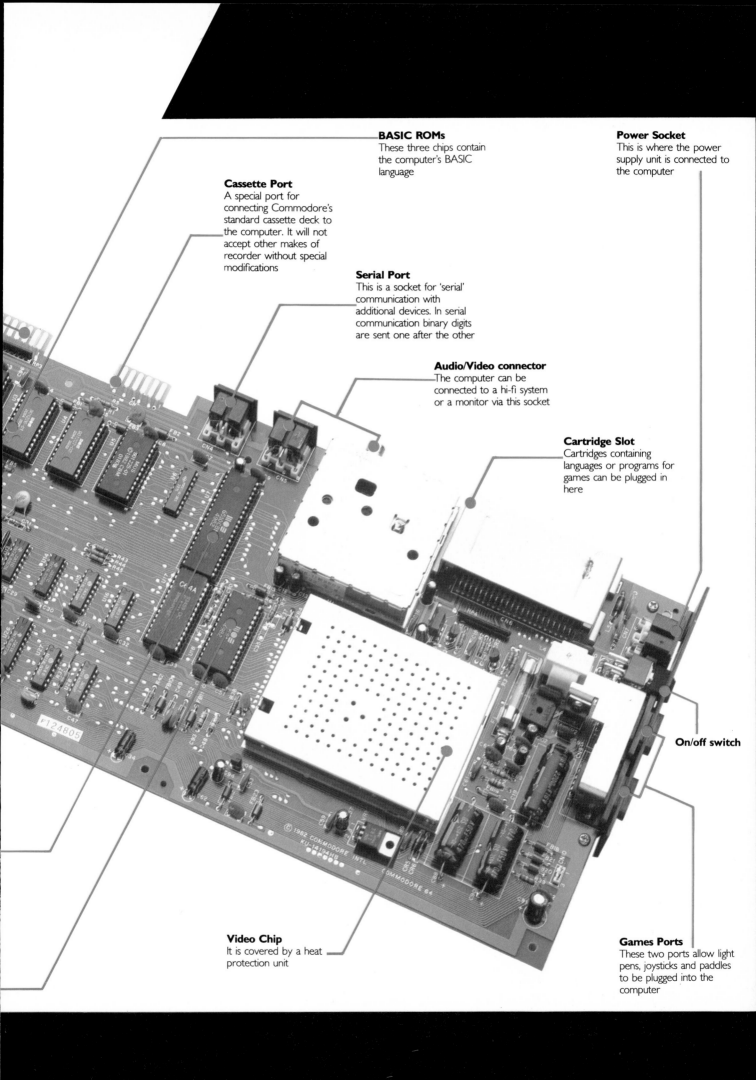

BASIC ROMs
These three chips contain the computer's BASIC language

Power Socket
This is where the power supply unit is connected to the computer

Cassette Port
A special port for connecting Commodore's standard cassette deck to the computer. It will not accept other makes of recorder without special modifications

Serial Port
This is a socket for 'serial' communication with additional devices. In serial communication binary digits are sent one after the other

Audio/Video connector
The computer can be connected to a hi-fi system or a monitor via this socket

Cartridge Slot
Cartridges containing languages or programs for games can be plugged in here

On/off switch

Video Chip
It is covered by a heat protection unit

Games Ports
These two ports allow light pens, joysticks and paddles to be plugged into the computer

2 THE FIRST COMPUTERS

THE EARLIEST ATTEMPTS

The history of electronic computers starts less than 50 years ago, early in World War 2. But many of the ways in which we use computers have their origins in the more distant past.

In general, we use computers in two areas: to help with arithmetical calculations and to control simple machines such as toys or washing machines and very complicated processes like the production of iron or the refining of petroleum.

▼ Two 15th-century German clocks, examples of some of the earliest reliable mechanical machines.

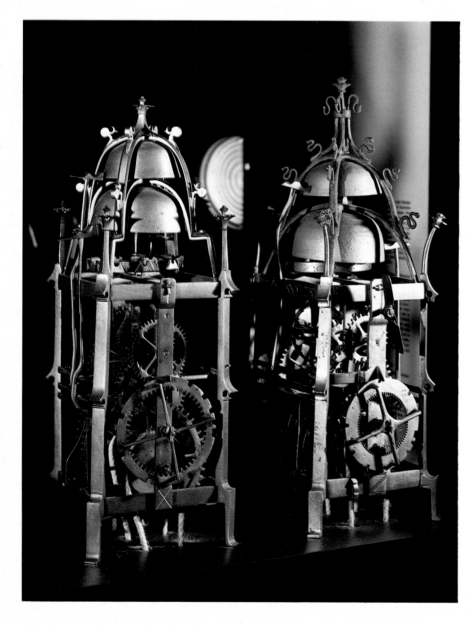

The clockmaker's art
Since the time of the ancient Greeks, 3,000 years ago, people have tried to make machines to do the simple repetitive tasks that are so boring. Perhaps the earliest examples of these efforts still in everyday use are the clocks in the great cathedrals and churches of Europe. In the Middle Ages cities and states vied with each other to have the most magnificent buildings, the most beautiful windows, the loudest, clearest bells and the clocks that kept the best time.

Not content with complicated sequences of bell ringing to mark the passing of each hour, the rich people of the towns and cities, who supported these churches, added mechanical figures – knights in armour, for instance, or mythical beasts such as dragons. These figures would emerge from the bell tower and do battle on the hour, every hour. They were controlled by a system of wheels and cogs, driven by the huge weights that drove the clock itself. The cuckoo clocks you sometimes see today work on the same principle.

Bells were not the only musical instruments to be controlled mechanically. Music boxes, with spiked drums or disks that plucked metal combs in a pre-set sequence to make a tune, were invented hundreds of years ago, and they seem to have inspired the earliest uses of mechanical control in industry.

THE CONTRIBUTION OF THE CLOTH INDUSTRY

The production of cloth was one of the industries to benefit from this control. The printing of patterns onto cloth did not start until quite recently. In the eighteenth century patterns were made by using different coloured threads, and choosing which of perhaps three or four would show on the surface at a time.

Punched cards

In 1787 a Frenchman named Robert Falcon realized that he could show the position of each thread – whether it was seen or hidden – by making a hole in a piece of card. Each row in the pattern had its own card, and each card contained a hole, or not as the case may be, for each 'stitch' in the row, depending on which thread came to the surface.

Binary numbers

Falcon was using the *binary notation* system without knowing it! Only his symbols were a hole or no hole, not 0 or 1 as they are in computers today.

Falcon's invention was improved over the next 15 years by another weaver, Joseph Jacquard. In fact, punched cards are still used to store information in a way computers can understand. But, thanks to the work of Herman Hollerith, they have been further improved.

▲ A weaver in 1876 using a loom designed by Joseph-Marie Jacquard. The punched cards controlling the pattern being woven are at the top of the loom.

THE FIRST CALCULATING MACHINES

Herman Hollerith

Born in Buffalo, New York, in 1860, Hollerith was only 30 years old when his punched card machines were selected by the United States Bureau of Censuses to help analyze the results of the US census in 1890. Hollerith discovered there were 56 million people living in the United States at that time (about one fifth of the number today) and, as he charged the US Government 65 cents for each thousand cards he processed, his invention made him a rich man over night. Years later, in 1911, he founded the company that later became IBM: the world's largest manufacturer of computers.

◄ Herman Hollerith (1860–1929) developed the rather crude punched card system invented in France in 1787 into an efficient method of holding information.

► During his own life, Blaise Pascal (1623–62), the French mathematician and philosopher, was best known for his writing on religious subjects. Today, however, it is his contribution to mathematics for which he is remembered.

► Pascal designed his adding machine, the 'Pascaline', when he was only 19. It worked well, but was not a commercial success – it was probably too far ahead of its time.

► Gottfried von Leibnitz (1646–1716) was another mathematical genius. As well as inventing calculus – a special way of calculating or reasoning – he developed ideas that were to help lead to the creation of computers.

► Leibnitz made many improvements to the Pascaline. He designed the 'Leibnitz calculator' so that a machine could now do multiplication and division, as well as addition and subtraction.

Although Hollerith was the first man to do arithmetic from information stored on punched cards, he was by no means the first to build a mechanical calculator or tabulator, as it was first called. If we ignore the abacus, the bead counting frame that had been in use in the Far East for more than 4,000 years, we must go back to France, some 50 years before Falcon and Jacquard.

Pascal and his Pascaline
In 1642 a mathematician and philosopher, Blaise Pascal, after whom a popular computer language is named, produced a small calculator called the Pascaline. This could add and subtract numbers, correctly carrying from one column to another in both operations. It worked on the same principle as the mechanical mileometer still found in many automobiles.

Gottfried von Leibnitz
Pascal's calculator could only multiply or divide by repeated addition or subtraction $(4 + 4 + 4 + 4$ is the same as 4×4 – both equal 16). It was not until 1673 that the first machine to perform all four functions was produced. Its inventor was Gottfried von Leibnitz (1646–1716) a German lawyer and diplomat. His invention was used in many desk-top calculators well into the twentieth century.

The work of Charles Babbage
All these inventions and discoveries played a part in the development of data processing – the mechanical processing of information. Remember that the most important part of the definition of a

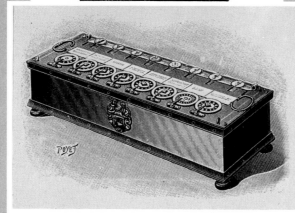

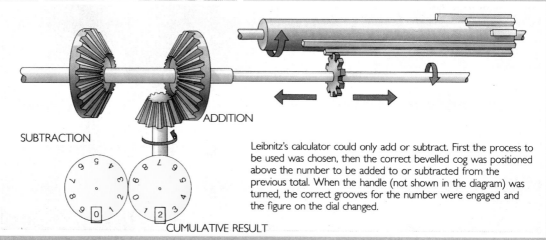

SUBTRACTION

ADDITION

CUMULATIVE RESULT

Leibnitz's calculator could only add or subtract. First the process to be used was chosen, then the correct bevelled cog was positioned above the number to be added to or subtracted from the previous total. When the handle (not shown in the diagram) was turned, the correct grooves for the number were engaged and the figure on the dial changed.

computer is that it can make decisions based on the information it is storing and act on those decisions. The first machines that could do this were designed by an Englishman, Charles Babbage (1791–1871). He first thought of using a machine to perform difficult calculations in 1812. By 1822 he had written an essay called 'On the Theoretical Principles of the Machinery for Calculating Tables' – he was referring to tables of logarithms, which had been in use since 1614 to make multiplication and division simpler and more accurate. By the next year, 1823, he had designed a small machine called the Difference Engine. This demonstration model calculated logarithmic tables more accurately than anything before.

The Analytical Engine

Babbage worked closely with Ada, Countess Lovelace (the daughter of the English poet Lord Byron) who was an excellent mathematician. In 1834 he unveiled plans for his Analytical Engine, which, though mechanical, worked on the same principles as a modern electronic computer. It could store information, make calculations, and most important of all, make decisions based on that information and act on them – all the qualities needed in a computer.

Unfortunately, the Analytical Engine was so far ahead of its time that it was impossible to build. In Babbage's time its thousands of moving parts could not be machined accurately enough, and although parts were built, the whole machine was never completed. If Babbage had lived in the twentieth century, it would have been quite easy to build his machine, and it would have been powered by electricity, not steam, which was the most advanced form of power in Babbage's time.

The role of electricity

Experiments with electricity had been made as early as 1774 when Georges Lesage, a Swiss inventor living in Geneva, built an electric telegraph machine to send messages from place to place. Other experiments followed and by 1851 people in Europe and North

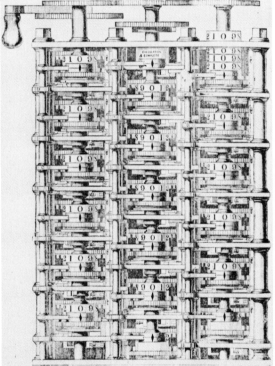

▲ Ada, Countess Lovelace, was an excellent mathematician and helped Charles Babbage (**left**) with the Analytical Engine.

◄ Sadly for Babbage, his Analytical Engine, which contained all the essential features of a modern electronic computer, was beyond the engineering skills of his time, and only a part was ever made.

America could talk to each other over a trans-Atlantic cable laid on the sea bed. But none of these early developments in the use of electricity to transmit signals from one place to another prompted the pioneers of computing to use the same methods.

Electricity was first used in computing to cause physical movement, by means of a relay, a remote-controlled switch that uses *electromagnets*. Relays are still used for switching appliances or circuits on and off, but their introduction into the successors to Hollerith's Tabulator made the computers faster and more reliable.

From these early machines and the things scientists and inventors learnt from them evolved today's computers. This is why you cannot really study the history of the computer without knowing a little about the work of men such as Pascal and Babbage.

▲ Part of the tabulator developed by Herman Hollerith to use with his system of keeping information on punched cards. The holes, 6mm (¼in) square were cut with special punches in different parts of the card to represent the different items of information. A tabulator is not a computer because it cannot make decisions about the information it holds.

THE FIRST COMPUTERS

We know for sure that the first computer was built by the second half of the 1940s, but exactly where and by whom is not so certain. Teams working in the United States, in Britain and in Germany all came up with the same ideas at the same time, but because of World War 2 (1939–1945), all inventions of this sort were closely guarded secrets.

Amongst the very first electronic computers were ENIAC, built at the University of Pennsylvania by Presper Eckert and John Mauchly during 1945–46; and Harvard Mark II (Mark I had been an electro-mechanical tabulator) built by Howard Aiken at the same time at Harvard University. In Britain, at much the same time, Max Newman and F C Williams built the Manchester University Mark I at Manchester University and a team headed by Maurice Wilkes constructed EDSAC at Cambridge University.

Probably the first machine to obey a program stored electronically inside itself, was the Manchester University Mark I in June 1948. This machine was later developed into the world's first commercial computer, the Ferranti Mark 1, which was delivered to customers in 1951, five months ahead of the UNIVAC which had developed out of the ENIAC project.

▼ The first computers were quite amazing looking machines! This is the original computer developed at Manchester University in 1948–49. The trailing cables and working parts open to dust and dirt are a striking contrast to modern computers.

▶ The *E*lectrical *N*umerical *I*ntegrator *a*nd *C*alculator (or ENIAC for short) was developed by the University of Pennsylvania in response to a request from an officer in the US army. It was presented in 1946. Although huge – it needed a room over 30m (100ft) long – it could only store 20 numbers of 10 digits.

THE TRANSISTOR ARRIVES

◀ The Manchester University computer (page 23) was quickly recognized as being a successful machine with practical, commercial uses. The Ferranti Company was given the task of developing a computer for sale. The photograph shows the Ferranti Mark 1 of 1951. Already it is looking more like a modern computer. There is a control desk for the operator and all the working parts are now behind doors, although three have been removed for the photograph. The machine is still large, there are similar 'cupboards' of working parts on the right, just out of the picture.

At the same time that these teams of scientists were at work on their computers, three men – John Bardeen, Walter Brattain and William Shockley, working for Bell Laboratories at Murray Hill, New Jersey, USA – were perfecting a device that was to revolutionize the entire science of electronics. They succeeded in 1947, when they produced the transistor.

Before the transistor, electric circuits relied on thermionic valves or vacuum tubes, which were very large, generated a great deal of heat and lasted only a short time before burning out. For example, ENIAC used 18,000 such valves and tubes and weighed 30 tons. Ferranti Mark 1 used only 4,000 but still needed 27 kilowatts of power – enough to heat two ordinary houses in the depths of winter! The invention of the transistor, which acts as a switch or an *amplifier*, opened the door to the IC (page 27) – the microchip that has made the microelectronics revolution possible.

▲ This is a photograph of a very highly-magnified transistor from the CPU – the heart of any computer.

◀ A company running a chain of teashops does not seem a very obvious pioneer of computers, but that was certainly the case with J Lyons and LEO (*Lyons Electronic Office*). Every day, the company's teashops handled hundreds of transactions and employed over 1000 clerks just to deal with all the paperwork. The company was aware of the research into computers being carried out at universities in the USA and Britain, but, unlike the universities who wanted machines to do long and complex mathematical calculations, Lyons needed a machine that could process an enormous quantity of simple data. When LEO became operational in February 1954, it took 1½ seconds to perform a task that took a clerk 8 minutes. LEO was such a success that other companies became interested, so Lyons decided to develop and manufacture LEO 2, an improved version (shown in the photograph). Later still, this was followed by LEO 3.

EARLY SOFTWARE

So far we have dealt only with the hardware of the computer: the actual machine, but there is more to a computer that that. In fact it cannot work without software: the Operating System (OS) and the programs.

The work of George Boole
One particularly important step in the development of software was the work of George Boole. Boole was born in the English town of Lincoln in 1815, the son of a shoemaker. He was the first person to realize that all our decisions can be broken down to a simple binary state: something is either true or it is false, in the same way that the light switch is either on or off (page 7). It is on this mathematics, called Boolean Algebra, that the principles of computer programming are based. We shall see how in Chapter 4.

3 ESSENTIAL BITS AND PIECES

At the start of Chapter 1 we saw how a simple switch can store a single bit of information: if it's up, it's off, if it's down, it's on.

BITS AND BYTES

Most of the computers found at home or in schools group eight *bits* of information together, to form what is called a byte. A single byte can hold an eight digit *binary number*. Each byte can store any one of 256 *codes*. This is a number in the range 0–255 – note that we start counting at zero, not at one! The computer treats every one of these 256 codes in exactly the same way, whether we use it to mean a number, a letter, a punctuation mark or anything else.

The character matrix
The characters displayed on the TV screen attached to the computer are all made in the same way. Each letter or number is generally made up of eight rows of eight dots. Each one of these rows is stored in a single byte, so it takes eight bytes to store the image of the character that will be displayed on the screen – we call it a *character matrix*.

The character is stored in memory as a series of ones and zeros. On the screen these appear as a dot of light, or no dot of light.

The 256 characters we have available for use are actually far more than we need, but the spare capacity is very useful if we want to make up symbols to use in games like Space Invaders.

Kilobytes
Because even simple computers need a lot of bytes of memory, we put them together into groups of about a thousand termed kilobytes (This word is often abbreviated to *Kbyte* or *K*.) When describing the size and capacity of a machine or a program we are more likely to say: 'It's got 64K of RAM', which really means 'It's got 65,536 bytes of Random Access Memory'.

Different ways of counting
This sort of shorthand is fine because it is universal, but why does 64K mean 65,536? It is due to the difference between counting in decimal and counting in binary.

In decimals, we progress in powers of ten – ten, one hundred, one thousand and so on. But in binary, we go up in powers of two – two, four, eight, sixteen and so on. But don't forget that in binary we also represent all numbers as different combinations of 0 and 1.

▶ A group of 8 switches gives 256 combinations of on and off. These switches are in position to represent X and Y in a computer using the *ASCII* code.

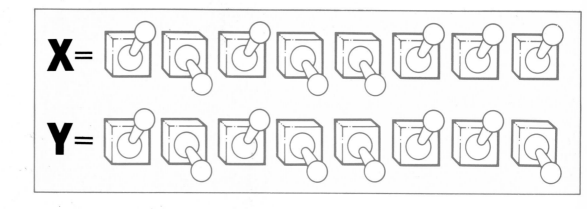

INTEGRATED CIRCUITS

In Chapter 2 (page 25) the invention of the transistor in 1947 was described as opening the door for Integrated Circuits (ICs). Why was this?

A transistor works as a type of switch. It can be turned on or off by applying a very small electrical voltage to it. Silicon, from which transistors are made, is naturally an *insulator*, but it can be made to act as a conductor too. Because it can be both conductor and insulator, silicon is known as a *semiconductor*.

Making ICs

The first stage in making ICs is to purify the sand to get rid of the oxygen and any other impurities, then to heat it in a special furnace to 1410°C (2570°F), so that it melts. Then it is allowed to cool slightly. The next stage is to push a rod with a small silicon crystal at the end into the liquid silicon. When the rod is withdrawn a single crystal of silicon up to 10cm (4in) in diameter and 2m (7ft) long will come with it. Each crystal is then ground down by machine until it is a perfect cylinder, and cut into slices 0.5mm (1/50 in) thick.

Even though silicon is cheap and easily obtained, slices like this still cost up to £12 ($15) because they must be very pure. The rooms in which they are made are even cleaner than a hospital operating room. One slice will make a hundred or more identical integrated circuits, and each one of these circuits could have the equivalent of up to 250,000 transistors in it.

The plan for the chip, designed and drawn with the help of a computer, is 250 times larger than the chip itself – and it is still complicated to read! This plan is photographed and then reduced in size. The surface of the chip, which has been polished until it is completely flat, is coated with a substance similar to the sensitive layer on photographic paper. The plan is then printed onto the chip, just as a photographic print is made. Because the circuits are made up of layers the process is repeated for every layer of the circuit, along with another

process that lays down aluminium to form the connections between one part of the circuit and another. Because this whole process can be done by machine, the cost is quite low, but more importantly the circuit can be kept very small, for the two reasons mentioned on page 16. The theory behind Integrated Circuits was worked out in 1952 by G W Dummer, a scientist working for the British Government. But it was not until 1958 that the first one was made, by Jack Kilby of Texas Instruments.

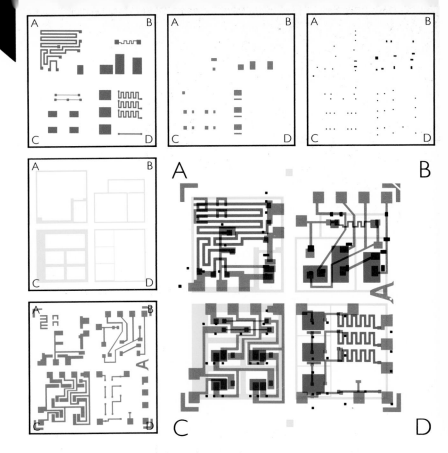

▲ Silicon chips are built up of different layers placed on top of each other – in the same way as colour pictures are printed. Here the four large chips are made up of five layers.

▼ A technician loads silicon wafers to go into a furnace for coating with the silicon dioxide into which each circuit is etched.

4 BASIC BASIC

▲ Thanks to the invention of the microcomputer, millions of people are discovering the fun and excitement of using a computer and writing programs.

▶ Variables allow us to make even greater use of a computer's powers of working with a great deal of information. In this diagram the variable is A, but to make the computer even more useful, A has a subscript (an extra description of the piece of information required). Here it is (X + Y − Z). Their values are shown in the boxes. So 5 + 6 − 7 is 4. Therefore A(5 + 6 − 7) is A(4). In this example A(4) is 20. So the instruction PRINT A(X + Y − Z) will result in 20 being shown on the screen. This gives greater flexibility than going directly to A4.

A(X + Y − Z)

5   6   7
X   Y   Z

A(5 + 6 − 7)
= A(4)

5   10   15   20   100
A(1) A(2) A(3) A(4) A(5)

The most commonly used *programming language* for microcomputers is BASIC. (Large computers can use a variety of languages.) It was made up in 1965, at Dartmouth College in the United States. The teachers there felt that the 'high-level' languages they had been using were too difficult for people who were not computer specialists, but who still needed to use computers in their work. BASIC is an acronym – a word made up of the initial letters of other words. It stands for *Beginner's All-purpose Symbolic Instruction Code*.

RESERVED WORDS

BASIC is very close to ordinary English. The words it uses, for example IF, THEN, AND, PRINT and GOTO mean the same in BASIC as they do in English. They cannot be used to mean anything else in BASIC. Such words are called *reserved words*. As well as these reserved words, BASIC uses the ordinary arithmetic signs and symbols (except that it uses * instead of × for multiplication, to avoid confusion.

VARIABLES

BASIC also uses code words called *variables* that hold the information needed for a program. Variables can have different names, depending on the program. You can make up your own names for them, too. But whatever name you choose it must obey certain simple rules:

Variable names must start with a letter of the alphabet.

They must not be a BASIC reserved word.

Some computers have a limit to the length of the variable name – but as it is usually something like 255 characters, it's not a problem. Others will recognize only the first one or two characters. This is more important, because we could call two variables 'AREA' and 'ARTICLE', but if we did, the computer would not know which was which because it would only recognize the first two letters – AR. There's one more thing to know about

variables – the sort of information that they will contain. In BASIC a variable name like AREA can contain only a decimal number. If it's a whole number, such as 15, it will be held as 15.00.

Variable suffixes
But we can add two suffixes to the end of a variable name – $ and %.

In BASIC the dollar sign, $, shows that the variable to which it is attached contains a string of characters. We can manipulate this string in a number of ways – take a number of characters off the front, or the back, or even out of the middle, but we cannot do arithmetic with the value of the variable. We normally use these string variables, as they are called, to hold alphabetic information, such as names, addresses and the like, but a string can hold any type of character.

The other suffix which can be attached to the names of variables is simpler. In BASIC, % added to the end of a variable name shows that the variable contains a whole number. If we try to put into it a number like 4.75 it will chop it off at the end of the whole number and show only the 4.

DIALECTS

When BASIC was invented none of the microprocessors that now use it had even been thought of. Unfortunately there are different versions of the language (sometimes called dialects, just like variations of the languages we speak) for every type of computer. A program written for one type of computer will probably need to be changed before it will run on another computer. This is why you have to read general books about BASIC and other programming languages along with the manual or handbook for the computer you are using. The main terms are, however, the same in almost all the various dialects of BASIC.

This is just a bare outline of what BASIC is and how it can be used on your computer. In the next chapter we will talk about programming and BASIC in action.

PROGRAMMING

In Chapter 1 a computer program was described as a series of instructions. There are three main types of input and output, which take information into the machine and give out the results; arithmetic and manipulation operations, which calculate the results and arrange the way they will look on the screen or on paper, and logical operations, that control the order in which the instructions are carried out.

WRITING A PROGRAM

The first stage in writing a computer program is a few short sentences that say very clearly exactly what it is we are going to do:

A program to find the average age of the children in my class.
Input will be children's ages.
End of input will be 0 or a negative number.
Each time an age is entered, computer will increase counter by one.
Each age will be added to the sum of those already entered.
When end of input is reached computer will divide sum of ages by counter.
Output will be average age.

Each of the individual steps in this program is very simple, so what we write to go into the computer will probably be much shorter than this statement of our aims. Computer 'languages', such as BASIC, are a sort of shorthand anyway and we use the symbols from mathematics to shorten them even more. We can make the code still shorter by using abbreviations of the names for our quantities or variables as described on page 29.

This is what the program to find the average age of the class looks like in BASIC:

```
10  LET SUM = 0: LET
    COUNTER = 0

20  INPUT AGE

30  IF AGE =< 0 THEN GOTO 70

40  LET SUM = SUM + AGE

50  LET COUNTER = COUNTER
    + 1

60  GOTO 20

70  LET AVERAGE = SUM/
    COUNTER

80  PRINT "THE AVERAGE IS ...";
    AVERAGE

90  END
```

Important numbers
The first thing you will notice about this program is that each line starts with a number, and that these numbers increase at each line. They do not have to go up in steps of 10, but it is helpful if they do in case lines need to be inserted later on. The numbers must be there so that the computer knows that it is going through the program in the right order. A program is a sequence or series of instructions and the line numbers control the order in which those instructions will be performed.

Reserved words
You will recognize a number of reserved words: INPUT, PRINT, GOTO and END, for example. Because BASIC is a beginner's language, its commands are easy to understand. INPUT tells the computer to expect information to be entered from the keyboard; PRINT in this case means display on the screen; GOTO causes a jump from one instruction to another, and END marks the end of the program, just as you would expect.

Variables

In this program there are variables: SUM, COUNTER, AVERAGE and AGE. We give the variables names by putting information into them. LET and INPUT are two ways of doing this. In this program:

LET SUM = 0 and
LET COUNTER = 0

means in everyday language:

Let the contents of the variables called SUM and COUNTER be equal to zero.

INPUT AGE

means

Take in a numerical value from the keyboard and store as the variable called AGE.

The most important part of the first statement is the equals sign. LET is only there as a reminder. In fact you may see:

SUM = 0.

This would work just as well.

It is important to remember that in BASIC, as in all other programming languages, there can only be one variable to the left of the equals sign. Writing something such as SUM + AGE = 24 will not work.

Although this program is only nine lines long, it contains all the important elements found in computer programs. Let's go through it line by line.

Assignment statement

Line 10 is an assignment statement – it gives (assigns) values to the variables called SUM and COUNTER. (In this program the SUM is a running total of the age of each child in the class and the COUNTER the number of pupils in the class.)

Input statement

Line 20 is an input statement, setting up the computer to receive some information from the keyboard.

Logical operation

Line 30 is a logical operation – the computer has to make a decision. It asks if the value just received from the keyboard is equal to, or less than zero. If the answer to that question is zero or a negative number, the computer will route

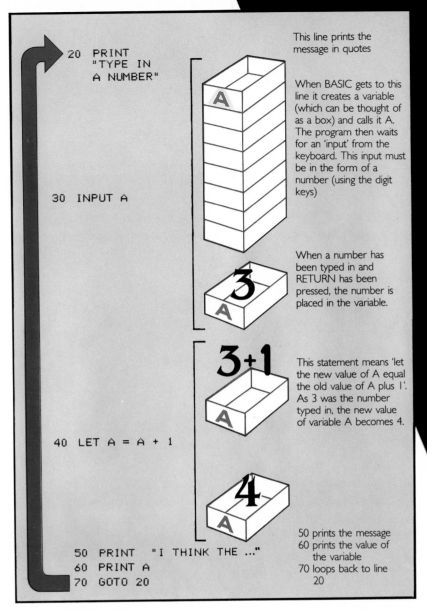

This line prints the message in quotes

When BASIC gets to this line it creates a variable (which can be thought of as a box) and calls it A. The program then waits for an 'input' from the keyboard. This input must be in the form of a number (using the digit keys)

When a number has been typed in and RETURN has been pressed, the number is placed in the variable.

This statement means 'let the new value of A equal the old value of A plus 1'. As 3 was the number typed in, the new value of variable A becomes 4.

50 prints the message
60 prints the value of the variable
70 loops back to line 20

the program straight to line 70, where it will work out the average age. If the answer to the question is a number greater than zero, the computer moves the program on to the next line.

Arithmetic statements

Line 40 is an arithmetic statement. It adds the values of the variables to the right of the equals sign and puts the answer in the variable on the left.

Line 50 is another arithmetic statement. Again it adds the values of the variables to the right of the equals sign and puts the answer in the variable on the left.

Command statement

Line 60 is a command statement, telling the computer to switch to a line other than the next one in the sequence.

▲ This very simple program shows how variables are used to store information (the variable here is A). It also shows how the GOTO instruction is used to form a loop back to the beginning of the program. Looping is described on page 32.

Another arithmetic statement

Line 70 is another arithmetic statement. In ordinary language it means 'Let the contents of the variable called AVERAGE equal the value of the contents of the variable called SUM divided by the contents of COUNTER'.

Output statement

Line 80 is an output statement. The phrase in double quotation marks, "THE AVERAGE IS ...;", will be printed exactly as you see it here, and the semi-colon following it tells the computer to print the variable AVERAGE immediately after it. If we had used a comma, the computer would have left some spaces between the two.

Line 90 is what it says: the END. Simple programs may not even have it.

Machine code

Now that everything is set up, the program can be run. BASIC is an interpreted language. This means the program is stored in the computer's memory in the same form as it is entered from the keyboard. When the program is run it is translated, line by line, and instruction by instruction, into the code that the computer itself understands. This is called *machine code*. It is possible to write programs directly in machine code and they will work much more quickly than ones written first in a computer language, such as BASIC, but writing them is slow and difficult.

So far we have dealt with the simplest of BASIC's commands. There are others, but mostly they are just even quicker ways of doing the same thing. Many of these commands deal with mathematics and trigonometry, others are concerned with character coding and decoding, while others are used with string variables. These string operations, in particular, change a good deal from one machine to another, so look them up in the BASIC manual for the machine. They will probably be called MID$, LEFT$ and RIGHT$, but some BASIC dialects do not have them all.

Looping

One important part of programming that we have not yet mentioned is *looping*. Looping means that you can go back to an earlier point in the program and do something again and again, as many times as necessary. There is an example of looping in our program. Line 60 is an instruction to go (loop) back to Line 20. In that program the computer went on accepting data from the keyboard and adding it in to the accumulator variable until it came to an entry that was zero or a negative number. This type of number is called a *delimiter*. A delimiter can be any number that is nonsense in the program, so that there will be no confusion as to whether the end has really been reached or not. That is why zero or negative numbers are often used. Another common one is 999, or, to make extra sure that there is no confusion, −999. Sometimes, however, you will know how many items you want to include. (In the example program it is possible that you would know how many children there were in the class.) If you do know the number, you can use a statement like this:

```
FOR F = I TO I0

PRINT F

NEXT F
```

This means:

While the value of F is between 1 and 10

Print the first value of F

Then print the next value of F, and so on until F equals 10.

This little three-line program will print all the whole numbers between 1 and 10, because the first line tells the computer to go through this loop ten times. But it might be more useful if the program did not have this limit of 10. Instead of the specific number 10 we could use a variable such as Y. For example:

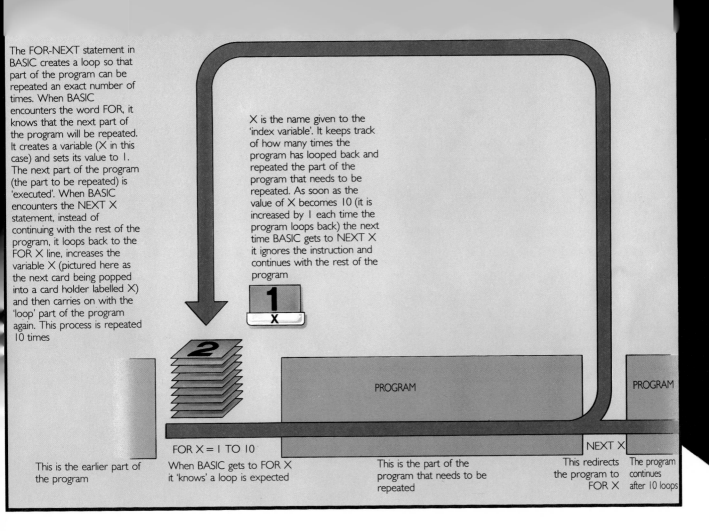

The FOR-NEXT statement in BASIC creates a loop so that part of the program can be repeated an exact number of times. When BASIC encounters the word FOR, it knows that the next part of the program will be repeated. It creates a variable (X in this case) and sets its value to 1. The next part of the program (the part to be repeated) is 'executed'. When BASIC encounters the NEXT X statement, instead of continuing with the rest of the program, it loops back to the FOR X line, increases the variable X (pictured here as the next card being popped into a card holder labelled X) and then carries on with the 'loop' part of the program again. This process is repeated 10 times

X is the name given to the 'index variable'. It keeps track of how many times the program has looped back and repeated the part of the program that needs to be repeated. As soon as the value of X becomes 10 (it is increased by 1 each time the program loops back) the next time BASIC gets to NEXT X it ignores the instruction and continues with the rest of the program

1 X

2

PROGRAM

PROGRAM

FOR X = 1 TO 10

NEXT X

This is the earlier part of the program

When BASIC gets to FOR X it 'knows' a loop is expected

This is the part of the program that needs to be repeated

This redirects the program to FOR X

The program continues after 10 loops

```
LET Y = 10
FOR F = 1 TO Y
```

But once again this limits us to the fixed value of Y. It might be more convenient to be able to change the value of Y every time we run the program. Then we would have to input Y instead of assigning (giving) it a value. In this case we would write:

```
INPUT Y
FOR F = 1 TO Y
```

Variables, arrays and loops
Variables can make it easier to enter lists of information. The example program shows that if we use a simple variable such as AGE, the contents change every time we go round the loop. But if we want to store the ages we are entering into the computer, perhaps to use later in the program, the system is slightly different. In BASIC we can set up a group of variables which have the same name, but use a number as well to make each one separate from the rest. For example: A(10). This refers to the tenth section (or *element*) of the variable A. In this way we can store each piece of information that we enter into the program. Once again a program is more flexible if the element is not a specific number. In this case we might write A(X). Below is an example of a program showing how a whole series of pieces of information can be entered very easily with this sort of loop.

```
10 PRINT "HOW MANY ITEMS"
20 INPUT X
30 DIM A(X)
40 FOR F = 1 TO X
50 INPUT A(F)
60 NEXT F
```

▲ In diagrammatic form, this is how the FOR-NEXT loop in BASIC works. It is very useful when a particular part of the program must be repeated a certain number of times.

In line 30 is a BASIC reserved word that we have not used before. DIM is short for DIMENSION and just tells the computer to set aside enough storage space for the number of elements in the variable A – in this case X of them. Using this approach we can rewrite the program to find the average age of the children in the class in the following way:

```
10  DIM AGE (50)

20  SUM = 0

30  FOR F = I TO 50

40  INPUT AGE(F)

50  COUNTER = F

60  IF AGE(F) =<0 THEN F = 50

70  SUM = SUM +
        AGE(COUNTER)

80  NEXT F

90  PRINT "THE AVERAGE IS ...";
        SUM/COUNTER
```

This is still a loop, but we get out of it in a slightly different way. When the text at line 60 encounters our delimiter (zero or a negative number), we will artificially reset the value of F – still at line 60 – to the value that we know will cause the loop to end.

What is the point of instructing the loop in this way? To begin with we have not used the GOTO statement. Even in quite simple programs such as this one, it is better to avoid it if possible. It is good practice for the future when you will be writing much more complicated programs. If you use GOTOs in them, you'll soon find yourself wondering exactly where you have to go to!

The other great improvement is that we have saved all the input data for later use. It is stored in the array variable AGE(F).

Saving time
You will also notice that we have telescoped the last three lines, compared with the original program. In line 90 of this program we just printed the result of the calculation SUM divided by COUNTER, although in the first program we calculated it, assigned the answer to a variable and then printed the variable. Both ways are acceptable, the second way is just quicker, although the value of average is not stored for later use. And when you start doing really long, complicated programs speed will be a very important consideration.

'USER FRIENDLY' PROGRAMS

In this look at basic programming there is one more thing to consider – how to make the program easier for other people to use. Doing so will make our program longer, so it will occupy more space in the computer, and because it is longer it will also be a little slower, though not enough to be inconvenient. Even so, until microcomputers were invented, these were both important factors, and the result was that, to use a computer, you would have needed a book of operating instructions. But now those instructions can be incorporated into the program itself, making it what is known as 'user friendly'.

Adding lines
At line 40 our program will be waiting for a person's age to be entered from the keyboard, so we should print a message that says just that:

```
33  PRINT "ENTER A PERSON'S
        AGE"
```

Now you can see why we numbered the lines in steps of ten! And how about ending the input stage? We went to some trouble to make the program flexible, so we'd better explain that to the user with a line or two:

```
5 PRINT "THIS PROGRAM
  FINDS THE AVERAGE AGE"

6 PRINT "OF UP TO FIFTY
  PEOPLE."

7 PRINT "WHEN YOU HAVE
  FINISHED, ENTER"

8 PRINT "ZERO OR A
  NEGATIVE NUMBER"

9 PRINT "WHEN YOU'RE
  ASKED FOR A PERSON'S
  AGE."
```

This time there is no need to leave gaps between the line numbers, because we know there will be nothing else to add.

The final improvement is to allow the user to run the program again, and we can do that by adding five lines to the end:

```
100 PRINT "DO YOU WANT TO
    RUN IT AGAIN?"

110 PRINT "ENTER YES OR
    NO."

120 INPUT R$

130 If R$ = "YES" THEN GOTO
    30

140 END
```

We can save time and space by combining the PRINT statement in line 110 with the INPUT in line 120:

```
    110  INPUT "ENTER YES OR
         NO", R$
```

and then leaving out line 120, and renumbering the later ones. We could do the same thing at line 40, instead of adding the PRINT statement at line 33.

FLOWCHARTS

The longer and more complicated a computer program is, the more difficult it is for the programmer to remember exactly what has already been done, and what there is still to do.

To make it easier, you can draw what is known as a *Flowchart*, or Flow Diagram. As the name suggests, a Flowchart is a picture of the way the program will go from one operation to the next. Each box in the flowchart is one operation, although that operation might be more than one single statement in the program. The lines that join the boxes indicate the way control passes from one

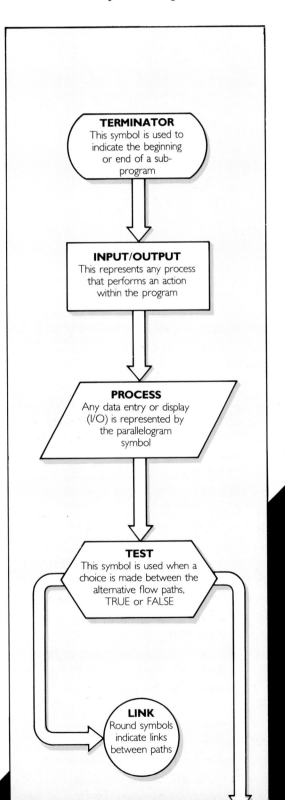

◄ Flowcharts only use five symbols, each one representing a certain part of the program. As the diagram shows, this is a fairly simple way of setting out a complicated program. (Sometimes a diamond shape is used for 'Test'.)

The four diagrams on this page show flowcharts in action.

operation to the next. This flow is always in one direction only – generally from the top of the page to the bottom, unless the programmer decides to branch to go back (loop) to an earlier point in the program to perform an operation again.

As you can see from the illustration, five types of box are used in a programming flowchart. Each shape has a different meaning.

An aid for programmers
As well as helping programmers to remember where they are, flowcharts give clear and simple pictures of the structure of the program: how the various parts fit together. They may not be important in a small program, but in a business program, or even a complicated game, they are essential.

They are also useful for another reason – it is much easier to 'read' a flowchart than a program, even one written in a fairly simple language like BASIC. So if you want to modify or understand a program that someone else has written, you refer to the flowchart.

Flowcharts are particularly useful when there are loops in a program. It is very important to organize loops properly and a flowchart helps us do this. The 'flow lines' must never cross. If this happens in the flowcharts, then we know immediately that we have made a mistake.

▶ Here the hexagonal 'Test' box shows there is a choice to be made. If X does equal Y, the program will branch to the subroutine. If not it will go straight to the next round 'Link'.

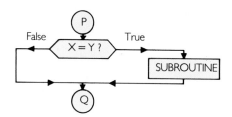

▶ The 'Test' box is also used if a loop is to end. Here, if the answer to the question 'AGAIN?' is YES, the program will loop back. If the answer is NO the loop ends and the program continues or comes to a stop, according to how it is designed.

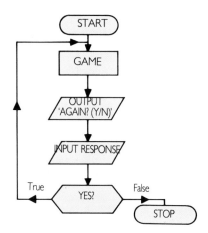

▶ A computer programmer working at the keyboard.

▶ Sometimes a program must follow one of two very different courses of action. Here, a player's score is compared with the highest previous score at the 'Test' or decision box. If the new score is the higher of the two, the program follows the right-hand Yes path, if it is lower it will follow the left-hand No path. The two paths rejoin where the highest score is output.

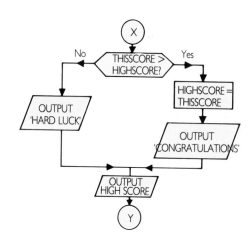

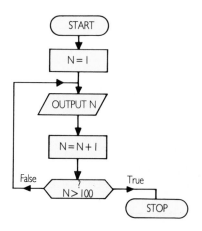

▲ This flowchart is designed for a program that will print out all numbers from 1 to 100. When N is less than 100 the program will loop back, but when N is greater than 100 it will come out of the loop.

6 COMPUTER SOFTWARE

A computer without a program is quite useless – it is just a very complex collection of electronic circuits. In many ways it's rather like a brand-new notebook without any writing in it. But not all the books we buy are empty notebooks. In fact, most are like this one, with words and pictures printed on the pages, and just as we can buy printed books, so we can buy programs ready-written for our computers.

BIRTH OF THE SOFTWARE INDUSTRY

In the early days of computers, long before home computers were invented, all programs were written by the people who used the machines and, in many cases, they were also the people who had built the machines. Later, computer manufacturers started to write what are known as *Applications Programs* to do the jobs that their customers wanted – wages, stock control, invoicing for example – and gave them away with the

▶ A computer cannot work if it has no program. Although it is fun to write your own program, it is often quicker and more efficient to buy a ready-made one. Programs, or software, are available for many different kinds of use, but a program written for one type of computer will not always work for another kind. The programs shown on the right are all available for home computers or other small computers. Most large companies with big mainframe computers have special departments where programs are designed for the company's own special needs.

Handle Words

Word Processing

With word processing software, your computer takes you one stage beyond the typewriter. Even good typists make mistakes, but with a word processor you can have perfectly printed letters every time.

The computer keyboard takes the place of the keys on the typewriter, the television screen substitutes for the paper in the typewriter. The words you type appear instantly on the screen, just as they do on the paper in a typewriter. But there the similarities end, and the power of the computer takes over.

Mistakes can be corrected instantly — on the screen. Words can be retyped or made to disappear. Even whole paragraphs can be deleted. Word processors do more than just delete words, though. If your thoughts could be expressed better by rearranging sentences, you can do exactly that, right there on the screen. The words or sentences you want to move around the 'page' are temporarily deleted (the word processor program takes them off the screen and stores them inside the computer's memory). They can then be inserted exactly where you want them.

When the document has been written exactly the way you want, it can be printed using the computer printer, or it can be stored on cassette or floppy disk for later use.

WHAT DO I WANT MY COMPUTER TO DO?

Balance The Books

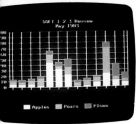

Accounts Package

Since computers can handle mathematical operations, it is hardly surprising that many programs are available to help the businessman. The range of accounting software is impressive, from automated bookkeeping to full accounting. Programs like these usually have to handle large amounts of information and need to store large numbers of records. Consequently they usually require at least one floppy disk drive to cope with the large storage requirements.

Accounting programs generally work through a system of questions (displayed on the computer screen) and answers (supplied by the computer operator). The information typed in by the operator is manipulated by the computer program, all the necessary calculations are done and the results are stored on the floppy disk or printed on the printer as appropriate.

Such programs include the automatic issuing of invoices, reordering of stock, keeping of ledgers and keeping track of work in progress. This software is expensive.

Filing

Databases

Computers can search through files of information far quicker than people can. At its simplest (and cheapest) a database may be little more than a computerised address book that can look up names, addresses and telephone numbers. More sophisticated and expensive database programs can perform far more complex operations.

For example, consider a botanist who is compiling information for a book on poisonous mushrooms. He will have extensive files on various species and their habitats. He may also have notes on a wide variety of reference books, and a list of individual specialists.

Before computers, this information would have been written out on cards and filed in a card index system. With a database program and a computer, the information can all be stored in the computer's memory. Using the power of the database, the botanist can get instant answers to his problems. If he needs to have a list of all the fungi ever recorded in France, the database can give it to him. If he needs a list in alphabetical order of all the books containing the word 'poison' or 'poisonous' and 'mushroom', 'mushrooms' or 'fungi', the database can give him that too.

Databases need to handle massive amounts of information and are usually available only on floppy disks. They tend to be expensive.

Handle Numbers

Spreadsheets

The spreadsheet is the computer's answer to all those 'what if' questions that used to be tackled with a calculator and reams of paper. Any business with a product to sell has many variables. Changing one generally affects most of the others.

Consider the questions a cinema proprietor might ask. "If all the seats were sold, how cheap could we make the seat price?" or "Would we get more revenue by reducing the price of ice cream with the same number of usherettes, or should we increase the price and employ two more people?" Each decision is likely to affect the entire business — lower prices may mean increased sales but lower profits. A spreadsheet can give instant results to questions like these.

All the essential numbers to be manipulated are arranged in a grid of rows and columns and the relationship between each row and column is specified (for example, the numbers in each row of column C is the result of subtracting the number in column A from the number in column B). Once all the real and hypothetical data is assembled, any single figure can be altered and the 'impact' on all the other numbers can be seen instantly.

The people who use spreadsheets are usually businessmen working out costings or engineers and scientists with very variable numerical data to manipulate. Speadsheets usually require both disk drives and a printer.

Entertain

Play Games

Computers are not only good for processing numbers and words. They can also provide many hours of entertainment if used with one of the many games programs available. These cover a wide range from chess and backgammon to arcade style games and simulations (such as 'lunar lander' and flight simulators). There are also extraordinarily complex adventure games that can take days or weeks to play.

Computer games are highly interactive. In other words, they require constant attention and input from the player. This input is usually via the keyboard; a key might be used to fire a 'laser' or a 'missile' or to control the movement of something on the screen. The number of keys used will vary, depending on the game and how much control the program requires.

A popular alternative to keyboard input is the joystick. These are plugged into the computer and operate somewhat like aircraft joysticks. They give greater control, and make playing computer games even more fun.

computers. They were all trying to make their computers more attractive than those of their competitors. By the early 1970s this had become a very expensive business – almost half the cost of the computer was in this software, and it was being given away free!

IBM, by far the biggest and most powerful computer manufacturer in the world, both then and now, decided to change all that. They decided to reduce the price of their computers, but start charging for the software that went with them.

Of course, while software was free, there was no point in people writing programs and then trying to sell them, unless the programs were very specialized. But as soon as computer users had to pay for their software, they became much more choosy. As a result companies producing nothing but programs began to appear and so the software industry was born.

Now that the majority of the world's computers are microcomputers, in use at home, in schools and in small businesses, the software companies have a much larger market for their products, and the programs they sell are much simpler and cheaper to buy. We can split them into two main types: games, which make up more than half of the sales, and 'business tools', such as Word Processing packages. Most games use the computer's TV display to show moving pictures, some part of which will be controlled by the person or people playing the game, sometimes from the keyboard but more often using a *joystick*.

TV GAMES

The first TV game was made in 1971 by an American named Nolan Bushnell. It was called Pong, and was a simple bat and ball game, a sort of electronic table tennis. From this small start Bushnell

▶ In the earliest arcade games, such as Space Invaders, players could only move their tokens along a fixed line. Now the 'maze chase' games such as PacMan and Battlezone allow players much greater flexibility.

▶ Astron Belt is an arcade game that uses laser disks to give a moving background when the game is being played. The images on the disk can be from real life or graphics drawn by the computer.

founded the Atari Corporation, which makes the sort of Arcade Games you see all over the world, as well as home computers.

Space invaders

It was not, however, until the first home microcomputers became available, that these games started to be popular. The earliest was Space Invaders, which has been copied many times since. Even computer games have developed their own language, and Space Invaders and the like are called Alien Zapping with Shields games.

Another popular sort are the Maze/Chase games. These started as a map of a race track of some sort, with a car that had to be steered round it. Games like this turned into the very popular Pac-Man, and the car race games turned into another type of driving game, where the TV screen actually shows an animated cartoon of the track and the player steers a car around using a wheel, accelerating, braking and changing gear as well.

Adventure games

The other popular sort of computer games, known as *Adventure Games*, started as books, with the players keeping score and checking that everyone played by the rules. The best known of these is probably Dungeons and Dragons. These games use mazes, too, but instead of showing the maze on the screen, a description of the place the player is standing appears on the screen. As well as getting from place to place, the player has to do things on the way – kill monsters, steal magic jewels and such, and is usually offered tools and weapons along the way, which he can take with him to use in the future, or leave behind. Some of these games can last for weeks.

In the last couple of years Adventure Games that use simple animated cartoons have started to appear, and we can look forward to the two main types of game being combined, so that you will be sitting on the flight deck of your own space craft, piloting it through fights with aliens and flights to other star systems.

◄ No need now to despair if your team loses – with a special computer game you can be sure they win every time. Or can you?

BUSINESS SOFTWARE

Millions of games are sold every year, and they are quite cheap to buy. Business software is a lot more expensive. The Word Processing program used to produce this book, for example, costs about 50 times as much as most games for home computers, but even so, it and programs like it are in use in hundreds of thousands of offices all over the world. There are software packages for every problem you can imagine, from keeping patient records at the dentist's, to helping a haulage contractor to work out the quickest route for his trucks.

◄ Farmers may not work in office blocks in cities, but they are in business in the same way as any other type of company. And the computer can help them, too. One very successful program works out the cheapest way to mix pig food so that the animals get all the nutrients they need at the lowest cost to the farmer. The program has sold to farmers from Mexico to Thailand!

► It isn't only huge international business corporations that benefit from computers. Small businesses such as a local chemist or pharmacist (**below**), with many different items of stock, will find it easier and more efficient to have the computer keep a record of what's been sold, what's in stock and what needs to be ordered.

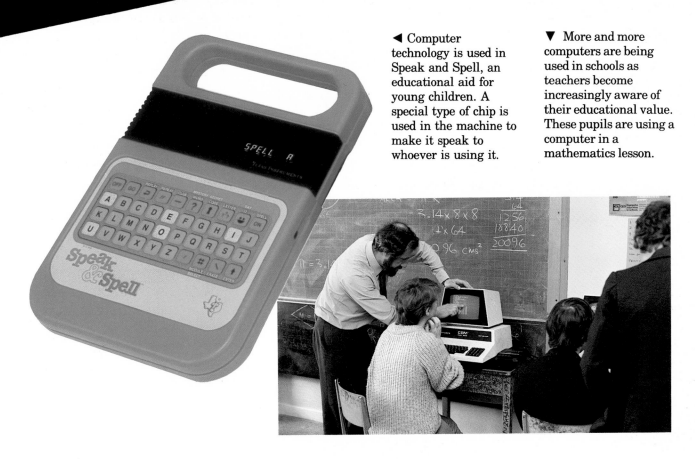

◄ Computer technology is used in Speak and Spell, an educational aid for young children. A special type of chip is used in the machine to make it speak to whoever is using it.

▼ More and more computers are being used in schools as teachers become increasingly aware of their educational value. These pupils are using a computer in a mathematics lesson.

There are two other important types of computer software: educational and operational. Educational software, as the name suggests, is designed to be used in schools. It is quite simple to have a written text presented by a computer instead of in a book. This book could have been made on cassette tape or *floppy disk*. But some people don't have home computers, and even if they do many of the computers cannot read tapes or disks meant for another machine. In schools, though, where the choice of computer is more limited, it is possible to use the computer like a text book. It is much cheaper to produce tapes or disks than to print books. Tapes and disks can also be 'interactive': they can ask the student questions as he goes along, and keep a check of his answers, so that the teacher can find out how much he really understands. Diagrams and drawings can be presented in this way, as well as written text.

SYSTEM SOFTWARE

The last type of software sometimes gets forgotten because it does not obviously do anything – except control the computer. This so-called System Software has to be in the machine before anything else can happen. Often it is recorded on an Integrated Circuit (page 27) as Read-Only Memory (page 13), and comes into action as soon as the computer is switched on. The programs – called compilers or *interpreters* – that enable the machine to make sense of programming languages like BASIC come into this group, and so do the Operating Systems. The average computer user never needs to worry about the way they work – indeed, they are difficult for all but the most experienced programmers to understand.

43

7 COMPUTERS IN USE

From being huge machines that used massive amounts of electricity and needed teams of people to keep them working, computers will now fit in a shoulder bag – and there is even a wrist-watch sized computer. And just as the computer has become smaller and cheaper, so the number of uses for it has increased.

A COMPUTER FOR EVERY JOB?

Of course, not every computer can do every job. Some jobs need really big, fast machines. Perhaps the best examples of this point are the computers used in space exploration, which have to work on thousands of different problems at once, and provide answers very quickly.

Space travel is not the only form of transportation to use computers. In a journey from New York to London, for example, as many as 24 computers may have a part to play, from issuing the ticket to remembering to order a special meal, briefing the crew, getting the aircraft into the take off position, guiding it through the air from one point on a flight map to the next, and so on through the hundreds of different operations that make up a transatlantic flight. And not only aircraft – ships, trains, trucks, cars, even motorcycles, are fitted with computers.

▼ Computers are turning up everywhere – not just in offices, schools or homes. This car has a computerised instrument panel – something that more and more car manufacturers are introducing into their new models.

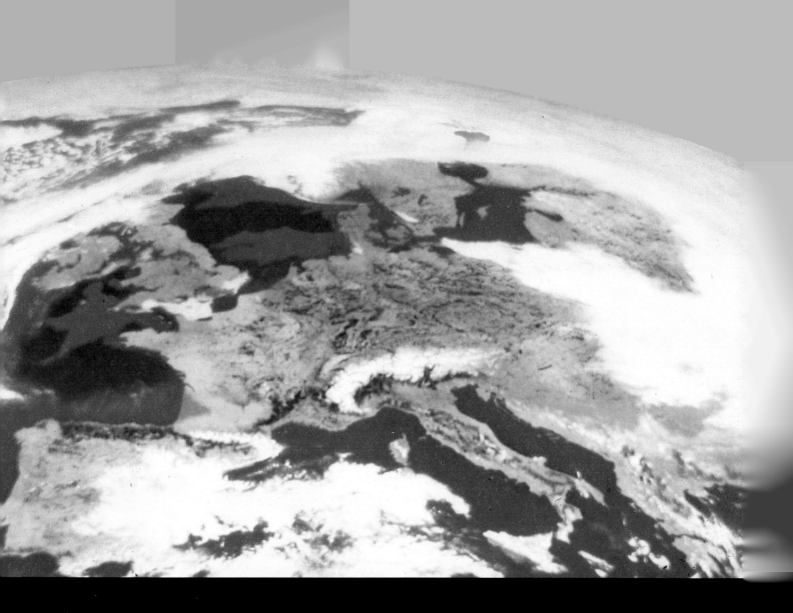

Weather forecasting

Another major use of large computers is very important to the pilots of those aircraft and the captains of those ships – weather forecasting. Using information gathered by satellites and from ground stations and buoys anchored in the oceans, weather forecasters can build up a picture of the atmosphere and weather over the whole of the earth's surface. Because there are so many pieces of information, each of them changing so quickly, it needs a huge, fast computer to deal with this information.

Animating films

One really spectacular use of computers is in the making of animated cartoon films – Walt Disney's 'Tron', for example. Animation relies on the eye being unable to see the change between one instant and the next, except as a representation of movement. The 'instant' in this case is

$\frac{1}{24}$ second, because that is the number of frames per second at which normal film is shown. When done by hand, animation is a very long and tedious job. For each sequence a background must be drawn and painted. Over that are laid transparent sheets called 'cels', onto which are drawn the figures that will 'move'. After that, each separate picture or 'frame' has to be photographed once. So, if there have to be 24 pictures for every second of cartoon film, even a five-minute film could take months to draw. And what about a feature-length film like 'Snow White', or 'Bambi'?

Using a device called a '*digitizer*' or 'digitizing tablet' (page 58), the artist can draw on a sheet of paper and have the drawing reproduced on the computer's display screen and stored in its memory. Some rather clever programming techniques then allow that drawing to be changed into another, so long as the

▲ This photograph of north-west Europe was taken by the Meteosat weather satellite, launched in June 1981 It is positioned some 35,880 km (22,300 miles) above the equator on the 0° meridian. Everything in the satellite is controlled by computers.

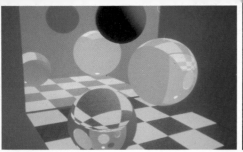

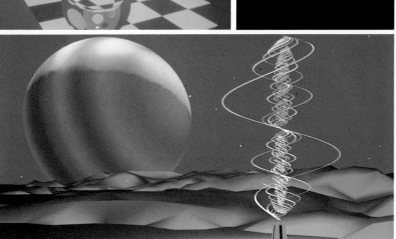

Three striking examples of just what it is possible to achieve with a computer in the way of graphics and 3-D simulation on a 2-dimensional screen.

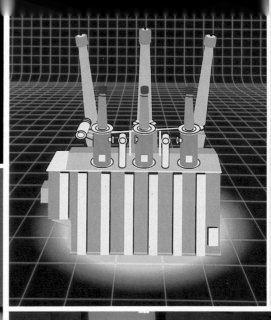

▼ If you think that the view from this pilot's seat looks a little unnatural you're right – it is part of a highly sophisticated computerised flight simulation training system.

▶ Thanks to computers the immense task of creating full-length animated feature films has been made easier and quicker. Keyboard, light-pen and VDU have replaced pens, pencils, paper and film.

computer knows what the end result is supposed to be. This process is quite similar to – though many, many times faster than – the way it was done by hand. The chief artist would draw the first and last frames of the sequence he wanted to animate, and juniors would then draw all the in-between stages. This 'tweening' as it is still known, was what took the time. Now the computer does it in minutes.

Simulating flight

Although film animation may not seem a very important use for computers, a similar technique is now used to train air crews. The latest flight simulators give the pilot and his crew an impression of what the view from the cockpit will be, and this is taken even further in the training of military pilots – because the computer holds a 3-D model of other aircraft and ground features such as airports and mountains. But the view through the windscreen is only part of this type of flight simulation. Most important is the computer-controlled movement of the cockpit mock-up, which responds to the movement of the controls in a way that feels just like the real aircraft.

MACHINE INTELLIGENCE

Much of the new work being done with computers now is aimed at creating so-called Machine or *Artificial Intelligence*. People who do not know about computers have always been afraid that these machines would one day be able to think for themselves. So far this seems unlikely.

It is, however, true that, given the information and good programming, the computer can come up with the right answer quicker than a person can – even an expert. In fact, *expert systems* are a special area of software.

EXPERT SYSTEMS

One of the areas where expert systems are particularly useful is medicine. They are used in hospitals and medical centres to help doctors decide exactly what is wrong with their patients. All illnesses and diseases show themselves in different ways – but there may be a dozen different ways or symptoms for any one illness. If the doctor can supply just a handful of observations, the computer can probably narrow down the possible illness so saving a great deal of time, and that may mean the difference between the patient living and dying.

Expert systems are in use in other jobs, too. Research scientists use them to check their results. Pilots use them to make sure of their position in the air. They are used to diagnose oil rig malfunctions. In the next ten years they will become even more common as they are developed for other areas of work.

▲American A10 ground attack aircraft on a bombing raid – or are they? In fact they are part of another computer simulation system for training ground- and air-crews.

▼ Computers can help in medical diagnosis. Ordinary X-rays give two-dimensional pictures, but if the patient's body is scanned by X-rays and the data collected on special sensors, the computer can build up a colour-coded picture like this one of a patient's head.

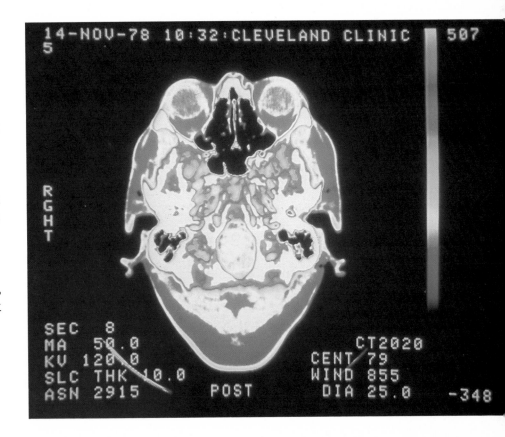

8 MORE COMPUTER LANGUAGES

BASIC is the most popular programming language for home computers and it is also widely used in schools and at work, but it is not the only one.

HIGH-LEVEL AND LOW-LEVEL LANGUAGES

You sometimes see BASIC, FORTRAN, PASCAL, FORTH and others described as 'high-level' languages. This means that they use words from ordinary spoken languages (almost always English), in just the same way that we do when we're speaking to someone else, so that we can understand at least some of the computer program when it's written down.

The other way to program the computer is to use a *'low-level' language* – assembly language or machine code. Low-level languages use simple codes that are much closer to the ones that the machine itself uses to store its instructions, and so they are rather more difficult to read and understand.

Why do we have these two quite different types of programming language? The high-level languages like BASIC are easy to learn and easy to use. Anyone can write a BASIC program within hours of starting to learn the language; a skilled programmer can write programs as fast as writing a letter to a friend. But when we come to use the programs, we find that they are quite slow. Not just in computer terms, where everything seems to happen almost at once, but even to the person using the program, especially if it uses the screen a lot to display information. A game like Space Invaders would be very slow indeed if it were written in BASIC on a home computer.

In fact most programs that you can buy in a store are written in machine code or assembly language. It is slower for human beings to work in than the high-level languages, even for an experienced programmer, but once the program is written it will run much, much faster through the computer. But although it is faster, that does not mean that machine code is always better. It is much easier to use BASIC if you want the computer to process lots of names and addresses, and other lists of words. And if you need to use fast screen *graphics* in the same program, most dialects of BASIC allow for a section of machine code to be included in the BASIC program, so giving the best of both worlds.

LOGO

To use languages such as BASIC, ALGOL, FORTRAN and PASCAL, you need to know something about arithmetic. But this seems rather contradictory if you think of the way quite young children can use computers.

Seymour Papert, of the Massachusetts Institute of Technology in the USA, realized that it is unnecessary for young children to learn a complicated programming language. So he designed one called LOGO, which does not use the same rules as the other languages. It is specially well suited to drawing pictures on the screen, or on paper or even the floor with a special sort of robot called a *Turtle*, that carries a pen around with it.

LOGO was not meant to be a general programming language, but more a way of helping children to learn about things in general. Many schools, though, are finding that it is a good place to start from if they want their children to accept the computer as a part of their everyday lives – which it will be, even if it is not already.

LOGO Logic

Here we show how shapes are built up on the screen using the LOGO language..

LOGO is a computer language developed specifically to allow young children — as young as four or five — to program a computer. It was developed at the Massachusetts Institute of Technology in the late 1960s by a team led by Seymour Papert, a mathematician who had worked with the world-famous educationalist Jean Piaget at his Geneva Centre.

For the youngest children, LOGO takes the form of a 'turtle', that is either a mechanical robot on the floor or a triangle of light on a computer screen. The command FORWARD 10 causes the turtle to move forward 10 units, drawing a line behind it. The command RIGHT 90 causes the turtle to make a right angle. Chains of commands can be built up that cause the turtle to draw squares, triangles, circles and unorthodox shapes as well. The turtle can be also taught to 'remember' the commands. Without realising it, children teaching a turtle are, in fact, programming a computer.

One way to draw a square box:

```
FORWARD 50
RIGHT 90
FORWARD 50
RIGHT 90
FORWARD 50
RIGHT 90
FORWARD 50
RIGHT 90
```

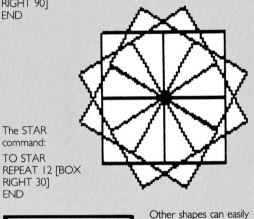

Constructing a 'BOX' command:

```
TO BOX
REPEAT 4 [FORWARD 50 RIGHT 90]
END
```

The STAR command:

```
TO STAR
REPEAT 12 [BOX RIGHT 30]
END
```

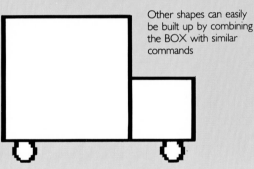

Other shapes can easily be built up by combining the BOX with similar commands

◀ Once, long ago, the blackboard was the most modern piece of equipment in the classroom! Now, in many schools, it is the computer. New equipment often means new methods of teaching and learning. The computer language LOGO was specially designed to help children become familiar with a computer. Then, when they are older and can think in the abstract way needed for most computer languages, the change will be quite easy because they are used to computers. It's rather similar to changing from very simple reading books with large print and simple stories to books with smaller print and more complicated stories.

▶ Turtles can be driven by BASIC, but they are generally used with LOGO. Controlled by a microcomputer, the Turtle, which is really a type of robot, trundles about on the floor and with a retractable felt-tip pen draws the shapes it is commanded to draw.

Although it can only move left–right, forward and back and the pen only goes up or down, teachers find it particularly useful in teaching mathematical concepts such as shapes, distances and the relationship between objects.

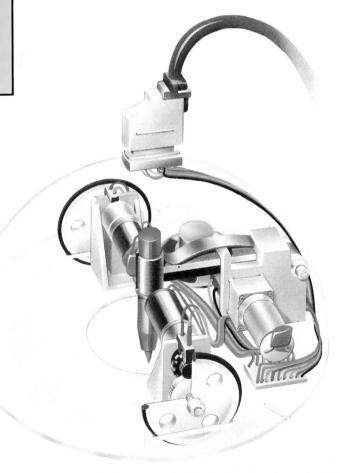

9 ROBOTS

In Chapter 1 we discussed the way computers look and how they are used to control other machines. The best example of this is the industrial robot. People have been interested in mechanical men, and perhaps a bit afraid of them, for thousands of years, but until the computer was invented no one had ever been able to build such a man. Even now, it is unlikely that anyone would – except just for the fun of it or perhaps for a film.

There are, however, thousands of industrial robots in use in factories in Europe, Japan, the USA and a few other countries. Most of them are used to make cars; some are used to move dangerous chemicals from place to place. In every case they help people by doing jobs that are dirty, dangerous and boring.

CONTROLLING ROBOTS

The hardest thing about controlling a robot is storing enough information in the computer about where the robot is and how it is positioned, and then controlling the motors that make the robot move so that it can go from one place to another. The motors themselves are quite special. They do not run and run as long as the electrical current drives them flows. Instead they move a certain distance at a time, in steps, and that is why they are called *stepper motors*.

There is a stepper motor for each direction in which the robot moves its arm (the robots themselves are usually fixed in one place), and these are switched on and off by the computer. The number of steps that the motor is told to move is stored in the memory of the computer controlling the robot, so that the computer always 'knows' where the tool or the piece of work on the end of the arm is located.

Imagine that the space in which the computer is placed is a hemisphere. The limits of the hemisphere are the maximum distance the robot can reach and the centre of the hemisphere is the robot's base. We can locate any point in that space by saying something like 'It's 18 steps forwards.' We do not talk about up and down, left and right, forward and back to the computer, but about X, Y and Z axes. The distance along each axis is negative or positive, counting from the mid-point, where all three values are zero. This is called the *datum* point.

Some robots have jointed arms, and that makes the job of programming them more difficult, because each joint has to be treated as a datum point.

PROGRAMMING ROBOTS

Two different programming methods are used. For *Follow Me programming*, someone who is very skilled at the job that the robot will do, holds the robot's 'hand', and just leads it through the job. Every time the person moves the hand, the movements are stored in the memory of the computer that controls the robot, so it can repeat them again and again. Usually the person will do the job three times, and the computer will take an average of the three.

The other method is slower, but more accurate. The human operator uses a control panel, telling the robot to move so many steps in one direction after another to arrive at the right place.

Some of the very advanced robots have a TV camera on the end of their arms and can recognize simple objects. They can pick the piece they want out of a selection and then place it where it is needed. Because they can go on doing the same job all day long, without sleeping or eating, and because they can work in places where people cannot go, areas of high temperature or pressure, for example, the use of robots will undoubtedly increase.

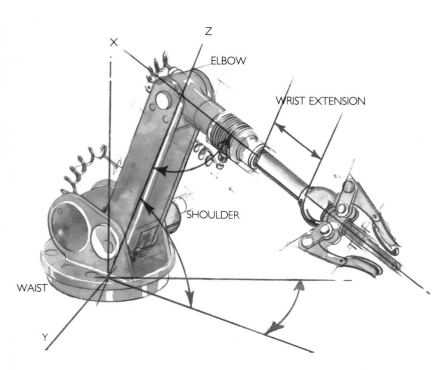

X Z
ELBOW
WRIST EXTENSION
SHOULDER
WAIST
Y

▲ Computers need precise instructions. Robots, too, need to be controlled absolutely exactly – after all, they cannot see if they have made a mistake. We cannot program a computer to make a robot move backwards or forwards, or left or right – that is much too vague. Instead we use coordinates on the X, Y and Z axes to provide the precise instructions the robot needs. However, when a robot has joints, a jointed arm, for example, programming is more difficult. The exact amount of movement each joint is to make must be worked out and written into the program.

Spools
The spools of string are arranged in such a way that if the shoulder angle is changed, the elbow angle will automatically change, to keep the 'forearm' at the same angle to the horizontal

Elbow
This has 270° freedom of movement

Forearm

Tension Equaliser
This pulley ensures that all three 'fingers' exert the same pressure on an object being gripped, even if it is an irregular shape

Hand
The three 'fingers' of the hand/gripper have spring-jointed knuckles, and rubber pads to help grip objects, when sensors are not fitted

Wrist
The wrist can bend through 180° and can also rotate through a full 360°

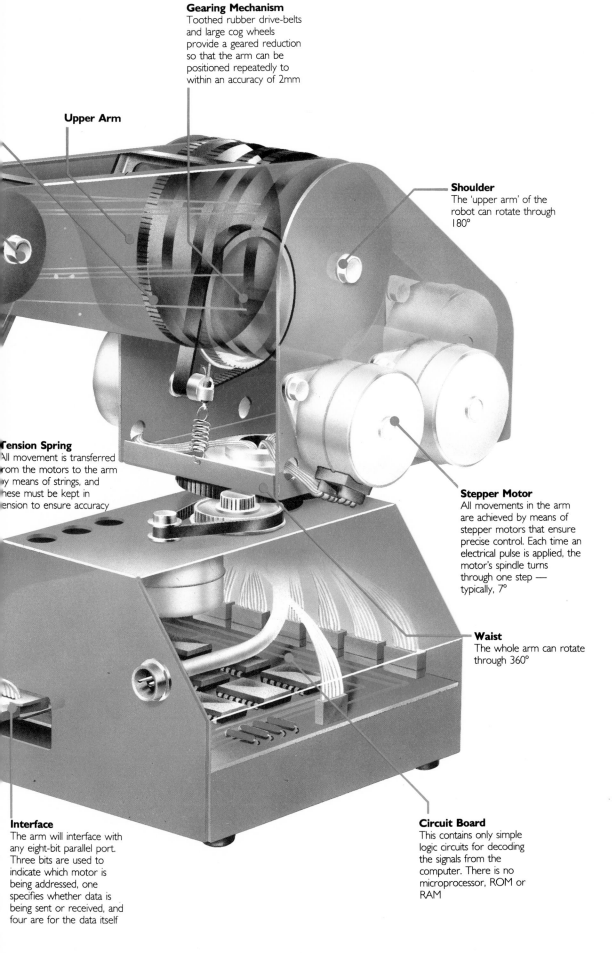

Gearing Mechanism
Toothed rubber drive-belts and large cog wheels provide a geared reduction so that the arm can be positioned repeatedly to within an accuracy of 2mm

Upper Arm

Shoulder
The 'upper arm' of the robot can rotate through 180°

Tension Spring
All movement is transferred from the motors to the arm by means of strings, and these must be kept in tension to ensure accuracy

Stepper Motor
All movements in the arm are achieved by means of stepper motors that ensure precise control. Each time an electrical pulse is applied, the motor's spindle turns through one step — typically, 7°

Waist
The whole arm can rotate through 360°

Interface
The arm will interface with any eight-bit parallel port. Three bits are used to indicate which motor is being addressed, one specifies whether data is being sent or received, and four are for the data itself

Circuit Board
This contains only simple logic circuits for decoding the signals from the computer. There is no microprocessor, ROM or RAM

◄ Surprising though it may seem, this robot arm is constructed on the same basic principles as the robots used in car factories, such as that on page 51. This 'Armdroid' has six stepper motors: one to rotate the arm at the 'waist', one each to control the 'shoulder' and 'elbow' joints and three to control the movement of the three 'fingers' in the 'hand'. Each motor has to be programmed separately and this information will be stored in the computer's memory. There is a further complication if the robot is handling delicate objects. If it is, the computer controlling it must be able to check the pressure of the 'hand's' grip. If it is too light the object will fall and perhaps break, if it is too tight it may still be broken!

10 COMPUTER PERIPHERALS

The computer on its own is a very powerful tool for solving problems, and can be used to play lots of interesting and entertaining games, but to use its power to the full other units must be connected to it. These units are called *peripherals*.

TAPES AND DISKS

Perhaps the best known peripheral, and the one that is most used with computers at home, is the cassette tape recorder. We can store information on cassette tape – it can be either programs or the data that programs will use, such as names and addresses – and use it to expand the memory of the computer itself. Instead of holding all the information in the computer's RAM, we can read in one record (a name, for example), at a time. The number of pieces of information the computer can then hold is limited only by the number of tapes we have.

Another way of keeping information such as this is to use magnetic disks. The recording method is just like the one used with cassette tape, but because the read/write head (picture left) that records or picks up the information is not fixed and can move over the spinning surface of the disk, each piece of information can be obtained more quickly than if we had to search through the whole length of a cassette tape.

Flexible disks – called floppy disks – can hold anything from 50,000 to 400,000 characters each side.

▶ The disk drive is one of the most useful of computer peripherals. It can both read and write information on a disk as well as find information stored on a disk extremely quickly. To do this the drive spins the disk at a constant speed as the read/write head goes backwards and forwards across the surface of the moving disk.

▼ A highly magnified picture of the head that reads and writes data on the surface of the disk. It is similar to the head on a cassette recorder, but is almost invisible to the naked eye.

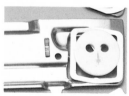

▼ Floppy disks are fragile, so follow the manufacturer's instructions carefully.

DON'T BEND   DON'T STACK   KEEP AWAY FROM MAGNETS   STORE CAREFULLY   KEEP AT ROOM TEMPERATURE

Analogue Board
This circuitry converts the signals coming from or going to the head. It translates the form used in the machine to the form that goes on the disk

IN USE ▶

Indicator

Driving Hub
This engages with the plastic disk and spins it round inside the envelope

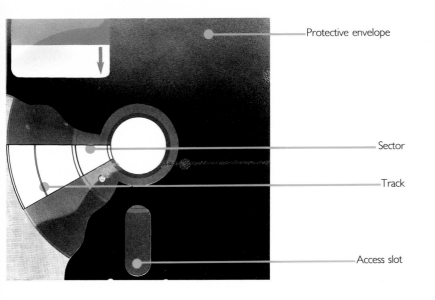

Protective envelope

Sector

Track

Access slot

◄ The surface of a floppy disk is divided up into a number of separate bands or tracks. These tracks are then subdivided into sectors. The disk, which is placed inside a protective envelope, is slotted inside a disk drive. Because a floppy disk can store so much information, each sector has an 'address' field so that each program can be located quickly.

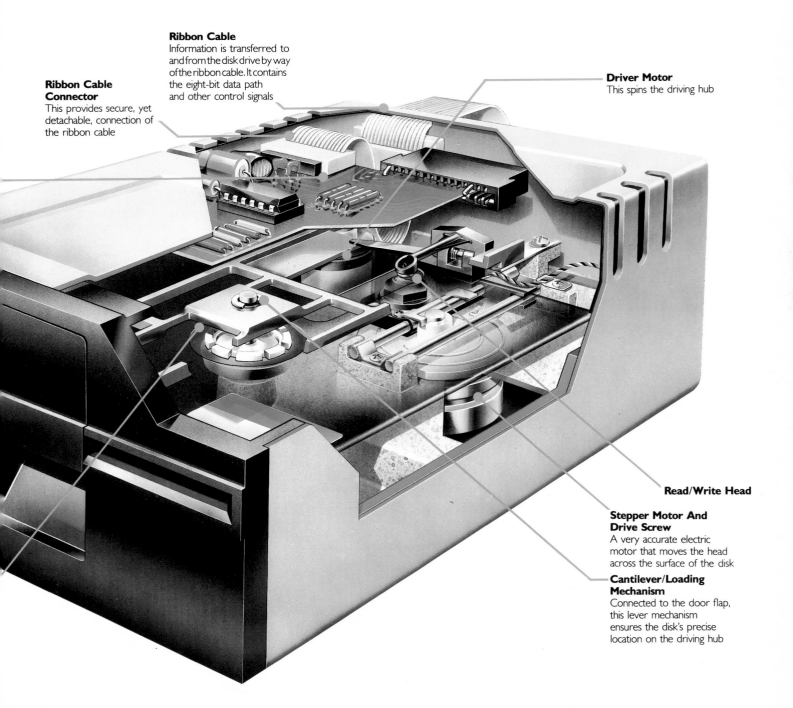

Ribbon Cable
Information is transferred to and from the disk drive by way of the ribbon cable. It contains the eight-bit data path and other control signals

Ribbon Cable Connector
This provides secure, yet detachable, connection of the ribbon cable

Driver Motor
This spins the driving hub

Read/Write Head

Stepper Motor And Drive Screw
A very accurate electric motor that moves the head across the surface of the disk

Cantilever/Loading Mechanism
Connected to the door flap, this lever mechanism ensures the disk's precise location on the driving hub

JOYSTICKS

Joysticks are often used by people who play on-screen computer games. When properly programmed, they cause the *cursor* (the square or line that shows where the next character will appear on the screen), or the token we're using in the game, to move about the screen, much more quickly than we could make it move by using the keyboard. A trackball, a ball a little smaller than a tennis ball, set in a holder that sits on the table, does the same job (see page 6).

▼ You won't find joysticks as part of a large business's computer system, but they're a great help in controlling missiles and aircraft in computer games!

Fire Button
In games this is used for launching 'missiles' or firing 'lasers'. In other programs the button can be given control over a single command

Potentiometers
These are often found in electronics where a voltage has to be varied. The volume or tone control in a hi-fi set uses the same principles.
 The potentiometers have a track of electrical resistance along which a 'wiper' can move. The amount of resistance in the circuit changes as the wiper advances. The computer measures the change in resistance and translates this information into a movement of the cursor on the screen. One potentiometer controls the vertical movement of the cursor and the other the horizontal

Cradles
The handle of the joystick is supported by these two cradles that are mounted at right angles. They are linked to the potentiometers. When the joystick handle is moved, the 'wipers' on the potentio-meters slide along and change the electrical resistance

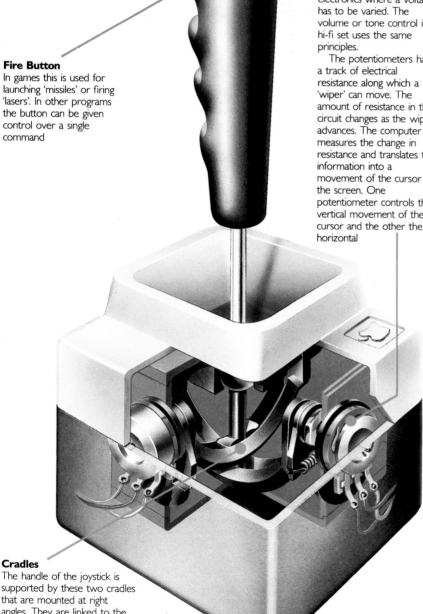

PRINTERS

Printers are almost always a part of the sort of microcomputer system that we would find in an office, but are not used at home so often.

 Printers are of three main types. Two of them print the characters as a pattern of dots, chosen from a rectangular matrix (page 26) and so are called *dot-matrix* printers. The cheaper of these two types use paper that is coated with a very thin layer of aluminium. The part that actually makes the dot is a tiny heated

Pen Bank
Up to three pens can be changed automatically. The gantry returns to the pen bank and exchanges the pen in use for the next colour required. Further colours can be exchanged manually

Magnetic Clips
These hold the paper flat on the bed of the plotter. They are made from a flexible magnetic material

PLOTTERS

element, that burns the aluminium coating where a dot is to appear.

The other type of dot matrix printer uses an inked ribbon, rather like a typewriter, and a set of fine needles. These needles press the ribbon onto the paper and make the character that way.

The third type of printer is much more expensive, and works in much the same way as a typewriter. The quality of the printing it produces is very high, and it is usually used with a *word processor*.

Character printers are not the only way to get your results on paper. *Plotters* and printer/plotters draw onto a single sheet of paper, using either ball-point or fibre-tipped pens. The pen is mounted on a beam, and both are movable, driven by the same sort of stepper motors used in small robots. The computer can send the pen to any point on the paper, either touching the surface so that it draws a line as it goes, or holding it just above the paper.

▼ The four-pen plotter/printer enables even home computer users to have inexpensive colour printing. This peripheral works rather like an ordinary printer, although different commands are needed to drive it. In this illustration you can see the instructions on the right. The paper on which the plotter/printer draws remains still while the horizontal lines are drawn, but for vertical lines the paper moves and the pen remains still.

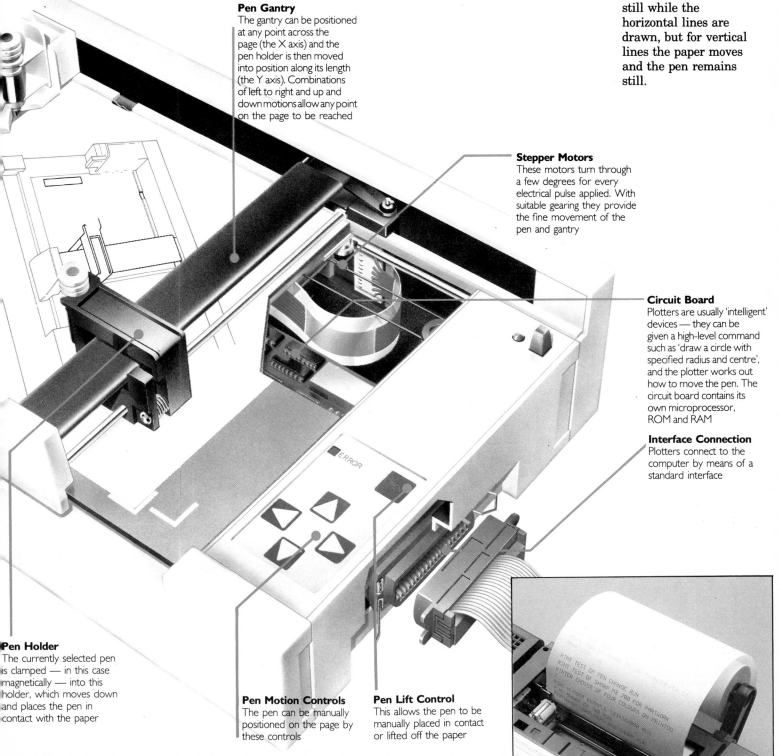

Pen Gantry
The gantry can be positioned at any point across the page (the X axis) and the pen holder is then moved into position along its length (the Y axis). Combinations of left to right and up and down motions allow any point on the page to be reached

Stepper Motors
These motors turn through a few degrees for every electrical pulse applied. With suitable gearing they provide the fine movement of the pen and gantry

Circuit Board
Plotters are usually 'intelligent' devices — they can be given a high-level command such as 'draw a circle with specified radius and centre', and the plotter works out how to move the pen. The circuit board contains its own microprocessor, ROM and RAM

Interface Connection
Plotters connect to the computer by means of a standard interface

Pen Holder
The currently selected pen is clamped — in this case magnetically — into this holder, which moves down and places the pen in contact with the paper

Pen Motion Controls
The pen can be manually positioned on the page by these controls

Pen Lift Control
This allows the pen to be manually placed in contact or lifted off the paper

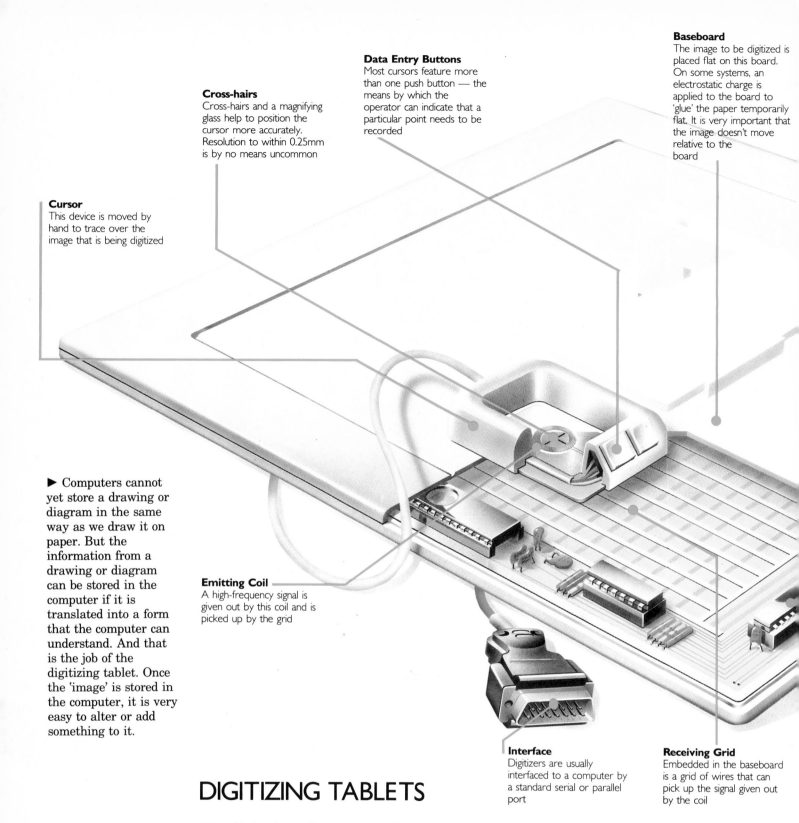

Cursor
This device is moved by hand to trace over the image that is being digitized

Cross-hairs
Cross-hairs and a magnifying glass help to position the cursor more accurately. Resolution to within 0.25mm is by no means uncommon

Data Entry Buttons
Most cursors feature more than one push button — the means by which the operator can indicate that a particular point needs to be recorded

Baseboard
The image to be digitized is placed flat on this board. On some systems, an electrostatic charge is applied to the board to 'glue' the paper temporarily flat. It is very important that the image doesn't move relative to the board

Emitting Coil
A high-frequency signal is given out by this coil and is picked up by the grid

Interface
Digitizers are usually interfaced to a computer by a standard serial or parallel port

Receiving Grid
Embedded in the baseboard is a grid of wires that can pick up the signal given out by the coil

▶ Computers cannot yet store a drawing or diagram in the same way as we draw it on paper. But the information from a drawing or diagram can be stored in the computer if it is translated into a form that the computer can understand. And that is the job of the digitizing tablet. Once the 'image' is stored in the computer, it is very easy to alter or add something to it.

DIGITIZING TABLETS

The digitizing tablet is something like a plotter in reverse. It looks rather like a small drawing board, but under the surface there is a network of fine wires running in two directions, so that they cross every centimetre or so. If you put a small electromagnet on the board and switch on the electrical current, it can be detected in the wires. Sorting out which pair of wires, one in each direction, has the strongest current gives the 'X–Y co-ordinates' (the position, in other words), of the magnet on the surface, in a way

which the computer can understand. Using the right program, a drawing on the board can be traced with the magnet, which need be no bigger than a pen, and, if you want, it can appear on the TV screen. Once it is in the computer's memory, it can be modified and changed.

LIGHT PENS

Another way of 'drawing' straight on to the TV screen uses a *light pen*. The TV picture is made by shooting a stream of electrons at the inside of the screen. There they hit tiny spots of a chemical called phosphor which glow. The stream of electrons is directed and focused into a bright spot by electromagnets inside the Cathode Ray Tube (CRT). The spot starts off at the top left hand corner of the screen, and travels to the right. The CRT turns it on and off as it goes so that it hits some dots of phosphor and not others. When it comes to the right hand side of the screen it jumps back to the left, one line lower down than before, and repeats the same process over again. There are many hundreds of these lines making up a complete picture (the number varies from one country to another), and the picture is 'refreshed' (the whole process repeated) 50 or 60 times a second. Imagine how fast the beam of electrons is moving across the tube! The light pen uses an electrical component that detects light. Point it at the screen, and it can tell the computer exactly when one of those tiny spots of phosphor is hit by the electron beam and starts to glow. A timing circuit allows the computer to work out where on the screen the light pen is pointing.

▼ Light pens are particularly useful computer peripherals for people working in engineering and design offices. They have the added advantage that keyboard use is kept to a minimum – in fact the user only needs to touch the keyboard if actual data is needed, such as the name and address of the client for whom the design is being prepared.

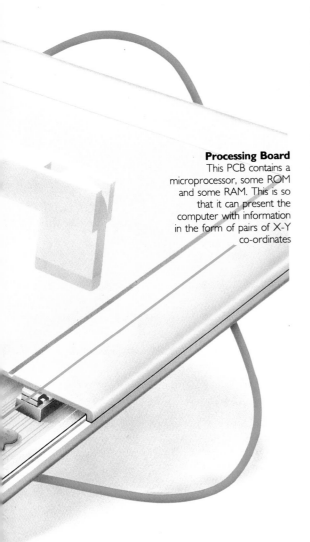

Processing Board
This PCB contains a microprocessor, some ROM and some RAM. This is so that it can present the computer with information in the form of pairs of X-Y co-ordinates

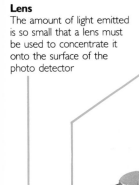

Lens
The amount of light emitted is so small that a lens must be used to concentrate it onto the surface of the photo detector

Photo Detector
This is a semiconductor device, which, crudely put, is like either a transistor or a diode with the top sawn off. Light falling onto this device controls the flow of electrical current through it

Amplification Circuits
These serve to detect and amplify current passing through the detector and send a suitable signal back to the video controller chip in the computer. Sometimes these circuits are housed outside the pen itself

Switch
Most light pens incorporate some sort of a switch, either operated by finger pressure or, in some cases, activated by pressing the light pen onto the screen. The switch is needed so that the light pen doesn't react to light (such as room lights) when it is not being used to select an item on the screen

Accumulator A special memory location in the microprocessor that stores data temporarily while it is being processed.

Adventure game A game in which the user plays one role while the computer takes other parts. It usually involves a series of rooms or caves to accumulate treasure while avoiding traps.

Alphanumeric A character that is either a letter or a number.

ALU Arithmetic Logic Unit. The part of a microprocessor that carries out arithmetic and logical operations.

Amplifier An electronic circuit that increases the voltage passing through it.

Applications program A program that instructs the computer to perform a specific task.

Array An arrangement of rows and columns in which numbers can be stored for easy access by the computer.

Artificial intelligence The ability of certain specially developed computer programs to 'learn' and incorporate their own 'experience' into their operation. (See also *Expert system*.)

ASCII American Standard Code for Information Interchange. A common way of representing the numbers, letters and other symbols that can be entered from the computer's keyboard.

BASIC Beginers' All-purpose Symbolic Instruction Code. The programming language used in almost all home computers, BASIC was specifically designed to be easy to learn and simple to use.

Binary notation The number system with base 2, in which all numbers are made up from combinations of the two binary digits 0 and 1.

Binary number A number represented in binary notation.

Bit Contraction of **Bi**nary digi**t**. A binary digit is one of the two digits, represented by 0 and 1, that are used in the binary number system.

Buffer A temporary storage area to hold information during transfers from one part of the system to another, for example from the keyboard to the computer's central processing unit (CPU). A buffer can be used to regulate the way data passes between devices operating at different speeds, such as a computer and a much slower printer.

Bug An error or fault in either a program or the computer itself.

Byte A group of eight bits, which forms the smallest portion of memory that the CPU can recall from, or store in memory. Its contents can be any binary number from 00000000 to 11111111.

Cassette Ordinary audio cassettes are used to store programs and data for home computers.

Character Any symbol that can be represented in a computer and displayed by it, including letters, numbers and graphics symbols.

Character matrix The group of dots on a display screen by means of which a single character may be displayed by selective illumination of some of the dots.

Character set The set of all the letters, numbers and symbols available on a computer.

Chip The tiny slice of silicon on which an integrated electronic circuit is fabricated. The term is also used to refer to the integrated circuit itself.

Code 1. The commands and instructions that go to make up a program. 2. Unique patterns of binary digits, representing characters or instructions, that can be stored in the computer's memory.

Coordinates Mathematical system used to fix position of something.

CPU Central Processing Unit. The component at the heart of any computer system that interprets instructions to the computer and causes them to be obeyed.

Cursor A movable marker, usually a flashing square, indicates where the next character is to appear on the screen.

Database A collection of data stored in a systematic way so that it is simple to retrieve or update any item or items.

Datum Unit of data.

Delimiter A piece of information of

known value, used to show when the end of an operation is reached.

Digitizer A device with which pictures can be turned into a sequence of digits and put into a computer.

Disk drive The unit that records information on the magnetizable surface of a spinning disk and 'reads' (recovers) information recorded on it.

Dot matrix A rectangular array of dots, commonly eight rows of eight dots, on which a character can be displayed by the selection of certain of the dots.

Electromagnet Magnet made by passing an electric current through a metal wire coiled around an iron bar.

Element One item in an array variable.

EPROM Erasable Programmable Read-Only Memory. Similar to the PROM, except that the memory contained in the chip can be erased using ultra-violet light and new programming recorded.

Expert system A system that stores facts about a particular subject according to the rules laid down by human experts. The system is capable of answering questions on its subject to the level of human expertise.

Floppy disk A flexible disk that is used to store computer data in recorded magnetic form, housed inside a protective square envelope.

Flowchart A diagram representing the steps of a computer program and thus the progress of a sequence of events.

Follow-me Programming One method of programming a robot, where the human operator takes the machine by the 'hand' and leads it through a job. The robot memorises each step.

FORTH A programming language intermediate between a *High-level language* and *Machine code*. By comparison with BASIC it is difficult to learn, but programs run much faster.

FORTRAN High-level programming language dealing mainly with mathematical formulae and used chiefly in scientific and technical programs.

Graphics The generation and display of pictures and images by a computer. The images are usually displayed on the computer's screen, although a permanent 'hard' copy can be obtained by using a special graphic printer attached to the computer.

Hardware The electronic and mechanical parts of a computer system.

High-level language A language like BASIC, which programmers can easily understand and learn.

Input Data and information supplied to the computer from its keyboard, cassette unit, disk unit or other input source.

Instruction A single directive to a computer to perform a particular operation. A collection or sequence of instructions forms a program.

Insulator Something that does not conduct electricity and so is used to stop the path of an electric current.

Integrated circuit/IC An electronic circuit that can consist of a large number of components and is formed in miniature on a silicon chip, typically a few millimetres square.

Interface A circuit or socket that connects two items of hardware so they can work together.

Interpreter A piece of software that translates one *high-level language* statement at a time into *machine code*, for execution by the computer.

I/O Input/Output. Equipment enabling communication of data to and from a computer. Also, the data involved in these communications.

Joystick A device consisting of a shaft that swivels on a base. When manipulated by its user it transmits signals to the computer, thus enabling it to control the movement of an object on the screen. Often used in computer games, the joystick sometimes has a 'fire' button.

K In the metric system, this represents 1000 (10^3), as, for instance, in kilometre (km) which is 1000 metres. However, since computers use the binary system (with base 2), K (written as a capital letter in this context) is taken as 1024, which is 2 raised to the tenth power (2^{10}).

Kbyte A unit of measure for memory size, being 1024 bytes (see *K*). Typical memory sizes for microcomputers are 16 Kbytes, 32 Kbytes and 64 Kbytes.

Light pen A device, shaped like a pen and sensitive to light, that, when moved over a display screen, allows the user to feed information to the computer. It works like a pointer and allows the computer to know which part of the screen is being pointed to.

Logic/logical The electronic components that carry out the elementary operations and functions, from which every operation of a computer is ultimately built up.

LOGO A high-level computer language. It is highly regarded as an educational aid, since it is simple enough to be learned even by very young children.

Loop/looping A sequence of instructions in a program that is executed repeatedly by the computer until a certain condition is satisfied.

Low-level language A programming language in which each instruction corresponds to the computer's *machine code* instruction.

Machine code The programming language that is understood by computers, because it is in *binary notation.*

Mainframe A large computer. In general mainframes have memories of more than 1 Mbyte and can work very much faster than home computers.

Matrix An arrangement of data in the form of a grid or a table, technically termed a two-dimensional array.

Mbyte A unit of measure for the memory size of a computer. It is 1024K which is approximately 1 million bytes.

Memory The internal store of the computer where programs and data are kept. The memory is divided into sections, each of which can be identified and accessed individually.

Microcomputer A small inexpensive computer containing a microprocessor. It usually has a memory of 4K to 64K.

Microprocessor A complex integrated circuit that can be programmed to perform different tasks. It is the main logical control unit in a microcomputer.

Operating System The software that controls and supervises all the internal operations of a computer.

Output Data and information leaving the computer; for example, the results of a program to be displayed on the screen, sent to a printer, stored, or sent to some other device.

PASCAL A high-level programming language.

Peripheral An accessory that, once connected, will increase the capabilities of a computer.

Plotter A computer-controlled device that moves one pen or more across a sheet of paper to draw pictures or 'write' characters.

Printed Circuit Board A sheet of plastic with metallic connectors formed in strips on it that link together the electronic components.

Printer A device for printing out text, results and program listings under the control of a computer. Some printers can also produce graphs and diagrams.

Program A sequence of instructions written in a computer language that, when executed, causes the computer to perform a required task.

Programming language A set of special command words and rules designed to describe to a computer how it should carry out a computation.

PROM Programmable Read-Only Memory. A chip that is programmable with the use of a special device, and then becomes a read-only chip, or *ROM.*

QWERTY keyboard A computer keyboard with its keys arranged in the same way as those of a standard typewriter keyboard. The name derives from the sequence of the first six letters of the top row of alphabetical characters.

RAM Random Access Memory. Memory in which stored information can be altered by the user. Its contents can be examined, or read, and also overwritten – that is, replaced by other information. This type of memory is known more accurately as read-write memory. The amount of RAM available determines how much memory the programmer can use to store programs and data. Dynamic RAM needs to be refreshed every few milliseconds to retain its contents. When the computer is switched off, the contents are lost. Static RAM retains its information.

Register A special memory location (often within the microprocessor itself) that is used for temporary storage.

Reserved word A command word

forming part of a computer language which, therefore, cannot be used, for example, as a name for a *Variable*.

ROM **R**ead-**O**nly **M**emory. Memory in which information is stored permanently. Its content can only be examined, or read; it cannot be altered. ROM is used typically to provide facilities that are always needed by the computer. The BASIC ROMs that are found in many microcomputers, for example, enable them to 'understand' BASIC.

Semiconductor A substance, such as silicon, that does not conduct electricity well at low temperatures. If heat, light, electric current or minute impurities are added it conducts electricity better.

Software The programs run by or associated with the operation of a computer.

Statement An instruction, or sequence of instructions, in a computer program.

Stepper Motor A type of electric motor used under the control of a computer that moves a known distance each time it is turned on, rather than going on moving until it is turned off.

Switch Device in a circuit that either allows electricity to flow in the circuit or else breaks its flow.

Subroutine A self-contained part of a program that can be called up and run by other parts of the program. It is usually written to perform a task that is needed frequently by the main program.

Transistor A simple Integrated Circuit that can work on its own as an amplifier or as a switch.

Turtle A wheeled mechanical robot (floor turtle) or a (usually triangular) shape on the screen (screen turtle), the movements of which can be controlled by commands from a computer.

Variable An item included in a computer program that can be identified by name, but whose actual value may be made to vary during the execution of a program.

VDU **V**isual **D**isplay **U**nit. The piece of equipment that provides the screen display for a computer. It is usually any ordinary television set or a specially designed unit called a monitor. The latter, though more expensive, will offer greater clarity and definition of picture.

Video The electronic signals and circuitry producing the display on a *VDU*.

Volt/Voltage Unit(s) of measurement of an electric current.

Word processor A combination of software and hardware for writing, editing and printing out letters and documents.

Acknowledgements
Bayerisches
Nationalmuseum
Munchen/Claus
Hansmann, British
Leyland, Kai Choi,
Commodore, Daily
Telegraph Colour
Library, Digital
Productions, Los
Angeles, Ian Dobbie,
Ferranti, Fiat Auto
(UK) Ltd, Bob Freeman,
Sally and Richard
Greenhill, HMG
Collection, W Howie/
Genigraphics,
Hutchinson and
Company Ltd, IMB UK
Ltd, ICL, Image Bank,
Kevin Jones, D Lister/
Ohio State University,
Tony Lodge, Ian
McKinnell, NASA,
Newbury Data,
Rediffusion Simulation
Ltd, Ann Ronan Picture
Library, Science
Museum, Science Photo
Library, Chris Stevens,
Texas Instruments,
Mark Watkinson, David
Weeks.